The Maui

Magical Mystical Tour

Kathy McCartney

Book Cover & Design by PIXEL eMarketing INC.

Art images for front cover and inside book by Kathy McCartney

Legal Disclaimer

Dedicated to...

My son, Ryan, who makes his mother proud. To be given a child to raise is a privilege, a magnificent calling and experience. What a blessing and honor to watch you grow into a wonderful man.

To the men and women who bravely serve and protect our freedom and great country. To the peacemakers of the world who stand united.

Acknowledgments

Many thanks to God and Mother Maui for allowing me to live my dreams here in paradise and for connecting me to my groovy soul family, who are visionaries in their own right and helped to inspire this book. To the many teachers I met on my path who taught me how to live and play again in the Haiku jungle and to the healing power of love.

To my family, whom I love unconditionally, my son, mom, dad, sisters, nieces and nephews, and my wonderful friends.

Mahalo to my photographer and friend Alek Mikolajczyk, who took the author's photos for this book. He captures the beauty in all he sees.

My sister Mary and her husband Jon Bilson for keeping our ohana and friends together every Thanksgiving. It is the best holiday gathering, filled with laughter and good cheer. You amaze everyone with your delicious, made from love, home style cooking! I don't know how you do it, Mary. I love you.

Raphael Sharpe for sharing his wonderful insights, wisdom, and stories. For his musical talents that he and Kutira share with the world.

Kutira Decosterd for calling together the beautiful souls in one magical place in time that allowed new friendships to blossom.

I want to give a special shout out to Patricia McCartney, Nanette Whitfield, Linda Compian, Ed Ellsworth, Julie Watts, and Erin Ramirez for taking the time to read the draft and for their mentoring, nurturing, and guidance on this project.

Mahalo to Melissa Se and her creative team for their invaluable assistance in editing and composing my book. She made the process easier to manage and complete. What a great team!

Contents

Introduction

Musings on Love

Love is patient. Love is kind (1 Corinthians 13:4). There is a man in the world that will love you the way you need to be loved. It is funny how distant these ideals become when we are faced with reality. My friend Jasmine once told me that "the grass in your relationship will only stay green and lush if you water it regularly; if not, it will die."

I have come to understand that this is true. Love is not a game between two people; it is a need, like air or water. Some people believe that the grass is greener outside of their partnership or marriage. They lose sight of what they have and start playing around in other people's backyards. Love naturally wants to prosper, but not when it has been replaced with envy.

Once envy steps in, a drought sets upon your garden, and it withers and dies. That is what happened with my fiancé Richard and me. One day I woke up from a suburban dream to discover that the love we had once shared had been replaced. My dream was an unconscious measure of my life, and it burnt to the ground the day I found him cheating.

Left with nothing but the drought of an apocalyptic aftermath, I left with my son and reunited with my parents in another kind of garden. At least I had support there. But the basis for everything I had once believed had been stripped away from me. I had lost faith in the love I needed to survive, and with that loss, a big part of my soul seemed deflated at the core.

That is partly why I decided to escape my imploded life and return to Mother Maui. For me, there is no lovelier, more beautiful, and more spiritual place than that island. This haven attracts sensitive souls searching for meaning, hunting for love and understanding at every turn. I knew I had to get back there, but I did not know how.

Maui is a place of love and spiritual investigation. If I was ever going to find the love I believed I deserved, it would be back home on Maui. I decided to leave it all behind: my parents, my sister, and my friends. My adult son had joined the Air Force and now he encouraged me to leave the nest and take flight like him. I needed to journey back to rediscover the love in my life. My spirit needed fuel like my body needs food.

I was on a mission to awaken love in my heart once again. How else could I recover from the choices I had made? Every person in the world needs to tend to their own garden. It takes time and tenderness. Love should flow and bring joy to you and those you share it with. I was hungry to find love again.

Only this time, I would guard myself. I made a pact that I would not sleep with any man while taking this journey to the Maui retreat. No sex at all. I would have to dig deep to find love without the trappings of attraction and physical comfort ahead of me. At forty-seven, a new chapter of my life would begin.

Chapter 1

Childhood Expressions

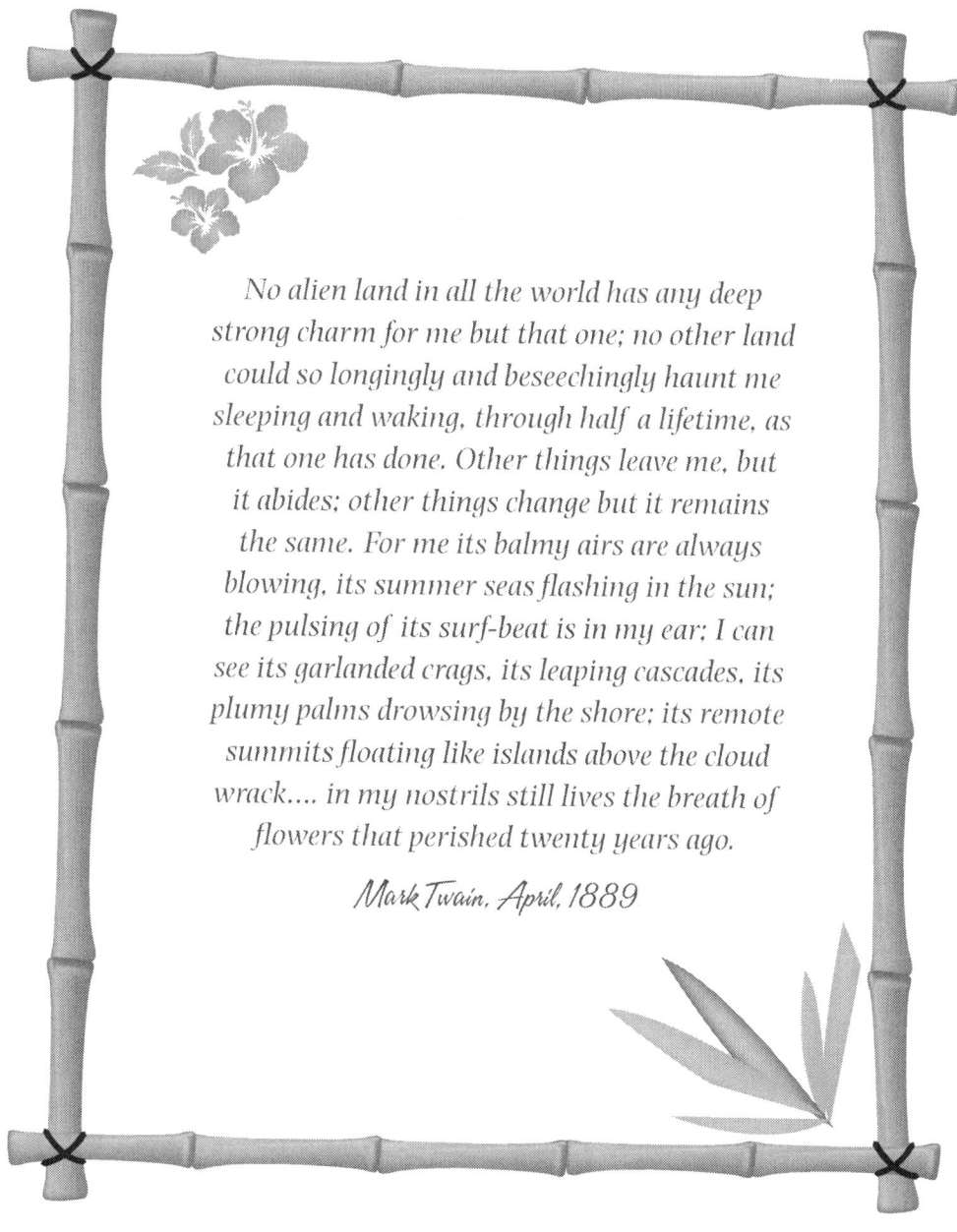

No alien land in all the world has any deep strong charm for me but that one; no other land could so longingly and beseechingly haunt me sleeping and waking, through half a lifetime, as that one has done. Other things leave me, but it abides; other things change but it remains the same. For me its balmy airs are always blowing, its summer seas flashing in the sun; the pulsing of its surf-beat is in my ear; I can see its garlanded crags, its leaping cascades, its plumy palms drowsing by the shore; its remote summits floating like islands above the cloud wrack.... in my nostrils still lives the breath of flowers that perished twenty years ago.

Mark Twain, April, 1889

Consciousness to the World Hawaii

I was born November 28, 1965, on the island of Manhattan, New York. My father was in the U.S. Navy, and he fell in love with my mother, a Taiwanese woman. I do not have many memories of those first years of life, not until we moved to a small military town in Kaneohe, Oahu, when I was two.

For me, life began in Hawaii. The endless white beaches were home, better than any snowclad landscape on the East Coast. I remember pattering across the wet sand with my bare feet, chasing the waves like a little Hunakai bird that plays with the foam at the water's edge. I would build sand castles in white sand that melted back into the sea, taking my dreams with it.

My seven-year-old sister Emily and I would spend hours swimming naked in that clear, turquoise water. It was an uncommon freedom.

The tropical breeze off the Pacific Ocean circulated the perfumed air and playfully tousled my brown wavy hair. The light mist lingered on my skin, forever captivating my young soul.

By age four, I was forced into kindergarten and I did not go quietly. I kicked and screamed and cried for my beach and my sand castles. Eventually, sand was replaced with school—although I never quite accepted that in my heart. Regularly, I would make my mother's life a misery by hanging on her like a deadweight as she struggled to drag me to the bus stop. Other days I would reluctantly comply, my head hung low, my eyes mournful and red from the tears. School meant clothes and conformity. I strongly disliked those things as a four-year-old.

I did what I could to be present at school, although my only memories of that time are dappled sunlight on gray stones, haloed clouds, and bright red flowers. My mind was always outside, back on that beach. I would get home from school and escape to the back yard, swinging and singing to Mother Nature. I had no idea about God back then but had a lingering sense that a higher power existed in the world all around me.

The day came when my U.S. Marine Corps uncle came to stay on Oahu with us. He was 10 years younger, leaner, and taller than my father, with bright blue eyes and light brown hair. Uncle Joel was not married and did not have any children. He later went on to play college football. That man was as kind as he was gentle. I threw a tantrum one day, and he soothed me in a way that neither of my parents had ever done before. He grasped my hand and walked me to the bus stop. I never threw a tantrum again after that.

Christmas on the Marine Corps base was my favorite time of year. All the box-shaped, neutral-colored homes would come to life. Families were allowed to hang lights and holiday decorations of their own. It was different. It was magical. It was the season for wonder and family.

I recall one home had a canoe on the lawn with a paper mache Santa Claus. My sister and I would sit in the canoe with Santa, staring at all of the wonderfully wrapped presents around him. Curiosity got the best of me, so I opened one of the shiny packages, disappointed to discover that there was nothing inside.

One Christmas I got a cool gift, a hot pink Cadillac car, made of metal, and it was powered by the "souls" of my feet. I would cruise the island with minimal supervision. Those were carefree days.

Each year, the military fire truck drove through the neighborhood with Santa sitting on the back. That Santa would throw candy canes off the truck for the kids to enjoy. My older sister Emily and I, dressed in our green hula skirts and bikini tops, followed the slow-moving fire truck everywhere like it was the pied piper.

We had magic powers, Emily and I. At that age, when you scratched the screen on the window during a storm, you were the one that made lightning possible.

As a young child, I loved to dress up in my mother's things. I would carefully don her favorite red silk traditional Chinese dress with Mandarin collar, put on her red lipstick, and then bolt outside. I wanted to run outdoors feeling beautiful and grown up in my mother's dress.

My sister and I loved to climb our jungle gym, fences, and tall trees. As a kid, I always had a lot of energy. I was very athletic, a tomboy by nature. Always a fast runner, I could outrun kids bigger than I was. I would run as fast and as far as I could but would always return home.

I loved nature and solitude. Our island home became a good friend to me. I did not know it back then, but my artistic soul found a kinship there that went dormant when we left.

California...Another Reality

When I was five, my family relocated to Southern California. I was not happy about leaving Oahu. Hawaii had become my home and my heart remained behind when we left. I had been kissed by the Aloha spirit and missed it terribly and nothing in California came close. I had to go to school all over again, only this time I left everything I knew behind. So I entered the first grade in So Cal absolutely clueless about numbers and letters, which my young mind did not comprehend.

My first grade teacher, Mrs. Album, had thick glasses shielding her pale blue eyes. She looked ancient to me. Her short, wiry hair was more orange than it should have been. Each day, Mrs. Album would call out a letter of the alphabet and do roll call. It was a nightmare. I did not know the alphabet or when to leave my chair. I did not know the letter K belonged to me. I will never forget Mrs. Album's stone-weathered face and the eyes of the other children, who turned to look at me as I walked nervously to the front of the room. At least she never corrected me in front of the entire class. I would just get up whenever the impulse struck me, on the letter P or perhaps J. Those short walks to the front of the class made me conscious of the fact that I could not read. I felt a little more out of place every day I had to do this.

I had to repeat kindergarten all right. My Hawaii education had given me nothing but dreams, and you could not sign your name in dreams in Mrs. Album's class. I had to move from the big school yard to the smaller playground on the other side of the fence. I was called names for being stupid. After an eternity, the first grade kids lost interest, and I had peace again. I learned young that crying only made things worse. Show any weakness to a pack of kids that do not know any better and vulnerability becomes an enemy.

I was a shy child. I would bury my face and body behind my mother's or father's legs in the hope that I would disappear completely when I had to meet one of their friends. Being shy became a liability, but it clung to me like a wet blanket. I did not know who I was without it.

Sadly, it lost me more than one great opportunity. I once had the chance to claim a first prize surfboard in a raffle, but I was too paralyzed with fear to respond. Going on stage in front of all of those people felt like the cool hand of death to me. I desperately wanted that surfboard too. But before my young mind could figure it out, I tossed the ticket away.

The announcer finally gave in and called out another number. On the way home, Emily told me that she would have gone up for me. It made me feel worse. From then on, I knew I had to work on lowering those shields that kept me a prisoner in my own life.

I loved to draw and create art, which is where I focused my confidence. My teachers recognized my gift and put me on special class projects. By the third grade, our library hosted its annual art contest, and I won third prize. I did a painting rendition of the book cover *The Best Nest*. I remember my mother scrubbing my dirty face, fixing my knotted hair, and whisking me off for the picture that the local newspaper wanted.

That was the first time I felt a rush of happiness and pride. Then again, in the sixth grade, for an art competition celebrating the 200th birthday of our nation. The other kids painted horses and battle scenes, while I chose to paint Betsy Ross, a seamstress, who made the famous symbol of our country, the American flag. It made an impression on the judges, and I received a first prize check for $25.00 and a world's worth of confidence in my art.

I grew up in a mostly white neighborhood, with the exception of the black family down the street; we were the only Asians in the area. At school, there was a Japanese boy but no one else. I remember worrying about the kids at school finding out that my mother was Chinese. It was my secret. My mother was a beautiful Chinese woman, petite with lovely, delicate curves and a pleasing face. Her dark olive skin and long black hair were distinguishing features, among many, that stood out. My mother often wore braids and reminded me of an American Indian, which I preferred over my own heritage. I still remember what they thought about Asians with the lyrics "Chinese, Japanese, dirty knees, look at these," with the final motion being to pull up their tops.

Then came middle school. I would not call it a living hell, because I felt dead inside most of the time. I would pray for hours that my breasts would come in, my butt would be curvy, and my legs shapely. I just felt like a human stick figure. I was short, skinny, and awkward. Sadly, my cuteness as a young child morphed into an ugly duckling phase.

My parents took it upon themselves to improve me at this time. "Katie, stand up! Sit up straight! Stop slouching!" my father would say to me. It did not stop the boys from saying terrible things to me. I had a big nose, big ears, knobby knees, and a flat chest. David, the most popular boy in class, flicked on my ears one day. I never wore a ponytail again. Many years later, at our twenty-year high school reunion, he was a little drunk and flirting with me. He said he did not remember me back then but sure wished he did. He was still immature.

Back in the day, white terrycloth drawstring shorts were all the rage. I bought them with my own money. One of the nastier boys told me I looked like I was wearing a diaper. I never wore those shorts in public after that. Having a body that developed slowly among girls who had sexy, adult figures was not fun.

My parents did not teach me about hygiene, so when my changing teen body struck, I had problems with greasy hair and odor. A friend at school introduced me to a razor and deodorant— what a revelation! It changed my life!

By age twelve I was working, ever the independent, enterprising spirit. I wrote plays, we sold tickets to our neighbors, and my sister Emily and our friend Patty acted the parts.

Babysitting was my regular job and bought me the clothes I wanted. With my earnings, I managed to go to the movies or buy school lunches. I saved most of the money that I earned out of necessity. My mother ran the family finances, and she did it with an iron fist. We only got Avon Products, socks, and underwear at Christmas time. The fun presents we got as little kids stopped when we became teenagers. Instead, my mother felt we needed practical gifts.

Living in Southern California in Orange County was rough for an artistic, awkward kid like me. There was so much pressure to be a tanned, supermodel-perfect girl. I constantly felt like a freak of nature.

I would stuff my bra with toilet paper to shape breasts for myself—a necessity before the wonder bra came out from Victoria's Secret. And what a wonder it eventually was for girls like me! One day during class, the toilet paper eased its way out of my bra and trailed out of my shirt. Hot and nervous, I covered my body by holding my chin to hide the trail. This took my complete focus, so I missed everything that was said in class that day. When the bell finally rang, I grabbed my books to cover my chest and made a beeline for the nearest bathroom for a quick readjustment. Toilet paper boobs were not easy to manage.

I did not understand at the time that my surroundings were what was wrong, not me. I lived in a shiny, packaged world of materialism, models, egos, movie stars, and mean teens. God wants us all to be happy as we are, but my surroundings and my peers made it impossible.

To make things worse, my emotional problems were always swept aside like I did not matter. "You know Katie, your father and I sacrifice a lot for you kids. We scrimp and save every penny to buy this beautiful house so you can live in this nice upper middle-class neighborhood. And you go to best public schools!" my mother reminded me in her thick Chinese accent.

That was enough to end any complaints I might have had. But a deep, gnawing sadness began to develop in me. When it got really bad, my mother would add, "Remember, be grateful for having eyes to see, ears to hear, that you not crippled, that you can walk and run, and that you healthy and not sick."

She was right of course, but somehow that did not make the sadness go away. There were times the dark spiral sank so deep that it threatened to overcome me. My spirit was torn to shreds, and I felt like a ghost among the living. I stopped believing in God.

I fell in naturally with the geeky, smart kids. They may have been unattractive and awkward like me, but they were silly and nice people. We spoke about art and philosophical things and would plot our revenge on the nasty, popular boys. An egged house or laxatives in a brownie was a serious plan at that age. A few of the good-looking girls were nice and enjoyed our artistic presence, and they helped us feel accepted in the end. It is amazing how much better a nod of acknowledgement from the right person can make you feel.

Middle school was like purgatory for me. Thoughts of suicide ran through my mind like my life was being subtitled. When I got really depressed, I would sneak a steak knife from the kitchen and run it across the skin on my wrist. I did not have the courage to do it, but I just wanted the pain to end.

By the time I got to high school, I was a master of running away from home. My parents' lack of sympathy and the open hostility that people in my life showed me was too much to bear. I disappeared for days to various friends' homes. I saw then how my upbringing was different.

Negative reinforcement is no way to raise a child. At sixteen, I got my parents' permission to live with a friend's family. I thrived there because I felt loved. I got better grades and achieved a B average. But when they wanted to adopt me, I said no. I could never hurt my parents like that.

Sheila, the friend I was living with, was blonde, busty, and confident in her youth. One day she got her report card—all F's. She sobbed hysterically, and as I tried to console her, she kept saying, "I'm in big trouble...." She locked herself in the bathroom and took a bottle of aspirin. I had to run to the neighbor's house for help. The paramedics came and pumped her stomach. She survived. After that, I had to return home; things were too heavy over at my friend's house for me to stay. My parents were relieved to have me back.

My Mother's Story

I could not blame my mother for how she raised me. She did the best she could, and times were hard. I once asked my mother about her parents, and she spoke to me very frankly about them, like the question confused her a little.

"We were taught children only have ears, no mouths. We were taught to listen and do what our parents tell us to do. So I do not know anything about my parents. Nothing personal because we were not allowed to ask questions. I can tell you your grandfather lost his eyesight when he was forty and had to stop working. He had glaucoma," she told me.

"But Grandfather owned a movie theater, didn't he?" I pressed.

"Before he went blind, movies were his favorite thing," she said softly. I could see a lot of pain there for her.

"What about your childhood?" I asked.

"When I six years old, it was World War II, and things were very hard. We had to run and hide; there were no hospitals, no schools. We hid in the mountains among Mandarin-speaking people, but I spoke Taiwanese, not Mandarin, so I had to learn fast their language in order to survive and make new friends. Then the Japanese occupied our island nation. Everyone was homeless, so we had to learn Japanese too."

"One night I play outside and saw a beautiful golden door appear in the sky. It opened. I called everyone outside, and together we pray. The door no stay open long. There was no time to wish for our individual wants, so we all pray for peace. The door closed, melted away, vanished. Then a miracle happened. Three days later, the war ended. There is a God," she said in her broken English as she released a long sigh.

"After war, there were no jobs, no food. Many had to beg to get by. I was so hungry; we had to eat bugs or rats or starve. There was a rice shortage; we had to stand in long lines for hours to get a pound of rice. Sometimes when you get to the front of line, they would run out; there would be no more rice." Mom paused and gazed up as if trying to remember more. She was eager to share her past with me.

"When I turn ten, I get a job; my parents tell me I am adult. If I want food to eat, I must bring home money to help family. I made powder for toothpaste and wrapped candy with wrapping paper. I good with my hands and developed knitting and sewing skills."

"There were no toy stores or grocery stores. But we had a black sheep, chickens, and a rabbit. I loved my animals; they were my best friends. They were better than toys. As they got big, one by one they disappear. My parents no tell me truth, that they had to sell them. They knew I would be upset. I would have fought to keep them."

"Then my dog got sick, and there were no animal doctors. Three times my parents drove my dog far away. Twice he found his way back home, sick, whining, and muddy. The third time, he never made it back. I cried for days my heart was so broken." I could see sadness in her dark brown eyes as she struggled at times to find the right words in English to describe her feelings.

"I went to school before I met your father. Then got married and moved to America. I taught myself English...and here I am."

It was true, my mother had experienced a very difficult upbringing. Born Ming, she was now Clara Ann McBride; she took an English name, the same as my father's mother. When she saw me looking at her with pity, she rebuked me. "We all have stories. But your mother is a very smart woman. I taught myself four languages: Cantonese, Mandarin, Japanese, and English and my native tongue Taiwanese. I taught myself how to type, paint, play the piano, and drive a car."

"I almost bled to death during my second pregnancy with a miscarriage, but I survived and had you in my third pregnancy, Katie, my number two child. You so stubborn and did not want to be born. Eventually you give in, and here you are."

She was a strong, independent woman, my mother, and a natural beauty with a 24-inch waist. She had long, black, silky hair and olive-colored skin with beautiful, dark brown, almond-shaped eyes and high cheek bones. My mother rarely smiled, but when she did, she revealed a movie star glamour with perfectly straight, white teeth. Most times she did not wear makeup except for lipstick to accent her full lips. If she wanted to be the prettiest woman in the room, she could easily have done it.

Once I understood my mother a little better, I tried to make it work at home. Knowing her past did not make our present any easier however. In many ways, it just made me more depressed. My parents had raised the two girls in the family with a very specific, strict ideology. This was especially prominent in our education when it came to men.

Chinese traditional beliefs from the past held men above women. I was raised to believe by society and high fashion magazines that my goal in life was to become sexually alluring, obedient, and good so that I could attract a successful husband. I was taught how to be submissive, even though all around me the world was changing. It was the era of the college-educated, powerful career women.

The '80s were a confusing time—enter large-scale divorce, confused family roles, and depression. I remember an Enjoli fragrance commercial from the late '70s with a strong, sexy, working career mother who did it all and still had enough energy to please her man.

The jingle went like this: "I can bring home the bacon, fry it up in a pan...and never let you forget you're a man...I can work till 5 o'clock, come home and read your tickety tock...and if it's loving you want, I can kiss you and give you the shivering bits." The slogan was "the 8-hour perfume for your 24-hour woman."

On the one hand, I had the world telling me submission to a man was wrong, and on the other, my mother was insisting that it was the only way, although she was conflicted too. Regardless, I slowly started to imagine a life where I could be more than just someone's wife.

My mother was an advice machine. She made it her personal duty to instruct her daughters well beyond what would constitute normal limits. When I was twenty-two years old, I visited my mother and will never forget what she said to me. "You should marry an Asian man, Katie. They treat you very, very good."

One day when my Korean friend brought me home after work, he briefly met my mother. "He is a good one," she told me once he had left. "Hang on to him, Katie. Is he Japanese?"

"No, Mom," I told her, exasperated, "he is Korean."

"Don't matter! Any Asian man is the best. They treat you better than a white man." My mother was a never-ending fountain of advice.

As a teen, I hungered for spirituality and was torn between my inexperience in the world and my endless curiosity. I created art, drew, and pondered on metaphysics and the grand unknown mysteries of the universe. I knew in my heart that there was more to this linear life than first became apparent. I was in a box, a prison—with four perfect corners.

People like me prefer a circle, a community of love and inspiration, not a rigid square based on someone else's perceived reality. I did not know it back then but that awkward, goofy kid had already started to adopt and reject some truths about this life.

One of these truths lingered around my feelings for the opposite sex. I was always passionate about men, and as I became a woman, I dedicated myself to learning the art of seduction. I was afraid of being used by men and was laden with the burden of Catholic guilt that I carried around with me, but this did not stop me from learning how to care for my appearance and how to be charming and demure, like my mother wanted.

Searching for the Fairy Tale

My mother's voice is still a staple in my heart. It was only much later in my life, in my mid-thirties, that I finally figured it out. I am sad to say that I married a man who did not deserve my attentions, and because of my beliefs, I stayed with him for far too long. My son saw a man mistreating his mother. That is something I cannot take back.

Later in my life, when I had to call my mother to tell her about my divorce, the advice came in thick clouds once again. "Marriage is especially hard in the beginning," she said to me in earnest. I sensed that she was right, yet I knew it would take two to repair my marriage. I felt like I was one short. My mother had hung on to her marriage like a rider on a bucking bull. Eventually, she wore herself and my father down. I wondered then if I could do that. If I could stomach the ride, with its ups and downs, bruised egos and tears. People did it all the time, right?

The truth was that I preferred to be bucked off, rolling away like a tumbleweed onto new horizons, wherever the wind would take me. At least then I would have a shot at real happiness. The purpose of the call was to let my mother know Sam and I were over, nothing else. Riley was eighteen months old, and I felt an urgency to leave Sam while Riley was still young.

"Are you sure about this?" Mom asked me. "Men mellow with age and mature. They slow down and become calm. Maybe you should wait...be more patient. He will settle down one day, just like your father." I saw into the future then, living with a man like my father. My parents had led separate lives under the same roof.

My mother still complained that my dad was not romantic. She was bitter about the sacrifices that she made and how little he appreciated them.

Despite that, she still encouraged me to stay. "You know Katie, your father never takes me out to dinner, to movies, or dancing." She often tells me how she deserves a trophy, but she is accustomed to hardships. My mother and father are comfortable and settled. They care for one another, but they live like roommates. I should have taken her advice on my wedding day all those years ago, when she asked me if this was the man I really wanted to marry. My heart said no, but I did it anyway.

Sam turned out to be immature and an abuser. We spent the bulk of our income on Sam's clothing so he could look like an executive. That was our way of investing in his career and our future. Being his devoted wife, I knew that one day I would benefit from the rewards. I took care of myself in other ways. I exercised and kept well-groomed but quickly felt like I was becoming less and less important. I allowed it without even realizing that a woman should always know her worth.

Now on my own, it was a challenge to find daycare for my son. Most facilities were full. We were placed on a waiting list. I found a nice woman who babysat in her home, but I still suffered separation anxiety from my son. He cried at the top of his lungs when I left him with a stranger. My heart was crushed as I turned to leave, hearing his wails and seeing his tiny back arch as he struggled with outstretched arms, pleading for his mommy. But there was no other choice. I had to work to support both of us. I wept in the car as I drove away.

I was armed with a high school diploma, some college, and administrative work experience. Macintosh and Windows PCs, like my son, were still in their infancy. The Internet had not yet reached critical mass. My next door neighbor had a startup company, so she took a chance and employed me. This was my big break.

I did not need a man or a husband to make it in this world and raise my son well. I took painting classes after work and practiced after my son went to bed. I needed my art. On the job, I learned about computers, sales, marketing, and the new world of digital cameras and imaging software. Most importantly, my exposure to others' quick successes helped me to believe that I, too, could become an entrepreneur. This entrepreneurial spirit shaped my future and served as the foundation upon which I built my dreams. I thrived in this exciting, supportive work environment. Creativity was encouraged, and everyone was a team player.

Having a young one to raise was challenging. There were sleepless nights, sicknesses, and just me to tend to everything. I was up to the challenge, however, because of my ever-increasing faith in myself. I knew in my heart that things would work out. I was late to work sometimes, bleary eyed as I put my briefcase down and climbed into the leather chair behind the big mahogany front desk.

I was the first face customers and prospective clients saw when visiting our image software company. This was the heyday of securing domain and .com names. Our posh office was vibrant, the walls scarlet, rich cerulean blue, and gold leaf. It was a place of inspiration, motivation, and fun! Nerds were in! Nerds were cool!

At the age of thirty-three, I purchased a charming two bedroom, two-bathroom condo in Pleasanton. This was the first time in my life I owned a property in my own name.

The World Wide Web and digital imaging technologies opened my eyes to a world of new possibilities, and five years later, I purchased my second home and investment property on Maui, Hawaii, via the Internet. I bought the condo sight unseen, at least physically. When I purchased my Maui condo, the numbers did not "pencil in." Many financially savvy people would have stepped away from the deal, and because of that I was a little scared, but I moved forward with the purchase anyway. This home was an investment in my vision and my dream that one day would lead me back to Maui. I started my own vacation rental business from afar while continuing to work full time at my office job in California. This was the first small business I created in which I was my own boss.

I became self-educated on methods of saving and learned to invest in stocks. I gained confidence and financial independence and started to build my retirement account. My fascination and interest in making money grew. I placed the maximum amount of my paycheck into my 401k; I learned that it is better to have your money work harder for you than you do for the money.

It is better to start saving and investing when you are young in order to have more time to multiply your money. I started at age thirty-one with a vengeance. I read financial articles during lunch or any break. After work, I faithfully watched educational money shows on PBS. As a single mother and woman, I learned that knowledge and independence are power and another form of freedom.

Chapter 2

Spiritual Calling

"Give me your tired, your poor,
your huddled masses yearning to
breathe free, the wretched refuse of
your teeming shore. Send these, the
homeless, tempest-tossed to me: I lift
my lamp beside the golden door."

The Statue of Liberty

The Tarot Card

Life is a spiritual experience. The signs are there when things need to change. My sign came suddenly one evening, quite by accident, and triggered a sequence of events that brought me back to Mother Maui sooner than expected. I was living with my third fiancé, Richard, a generous man who I thought was the complete package.

I had never truly been physically attracted to him, even when we first met. He was eighteen years my senior, and it showed on occasion. Richard was 5 foot 6, although he told people he was three inches taller than he actually was. His light brown hair had streaks of white frost above his temples and was styled youthfully, spiking at the top. It was thinning slightly and receding, revealing a broad forehead.

Richard had always been rather stocky and soft in the middle. He was not the typical man that I felt attracted to. It was his mental acuity, creativity, and confidence I liked. His generous heart, power, and jet-setting lifestyle did not hurt either. Richard wined and dined me, sweeping me off my feet as a single mother. Then it turned out he was a pleasing lover.

Things moved quickly once we became a couple. He lavished me with designer clothing, a new Mercedes, trips to places like Sofia,

Paris, Nice, Rome, Florence, Capri, Pompeii, London, Kingston, Brighton, Amsterdam, Brussels, Monaco and, of course, the Hawaiian Islands. We travelled in five-star luxury, and the lifestyle appealed to my free spirit.

After my terrible relationship with my first husband, Sam, Richard's charm, wealth, and stability were very appealing. Even though I was not attracted to him physically, I thought that true love depended on more than just looks and decided to take the risk. Looking back now, I can see that I settled. We used each other to avoid loneliness, although it was never enough for Richard. He hungered for attention in a way that I could not understand.

I guess men with money feel entitled to things from those around them. But I never signed on to be his housekeeper. And I definitely did not sign on to be his doormat. Inevitably, Richard's dark side crept up on me one day when he was in the shower and we were getting ready to go out to dinner.

The revelation hit me like a tsunami hits a high rise. Richard's phone beeped and delivered the end of my world.

"Check my phone, won't you, honey," his voice echoed from the bathroom.

I picked up his phone, and a message popped onto the screen—a message from a girl who worked as a barista at our local coffee shop. She looked like she was fresh out of high school, pink-cheeked and wild looking. As I read the text, my insides slid over themselves, forming a hard knot. I tasted betrayal, regret, and heartache in my mouth.

Hey Babes! Hot night last night, can't wait to do it again. Love the necklace, you're such a sweetie pie! Luv luvs, Candy.

That is what I wanted it to read. In truth, the content was far more explicit. The kind of words written by someone forty years younger than Richard. God. For a long while I sat on the bed in Richard's beautiful house too hurt to cry and too angry to speak. Then, as it does with selfish men, things got worse. He wanted me out. I suppose I felt that I would be safer with Richard as the younger, attractive one in our relationship, which obviously was not the case.

Just like that my plan for true love had imploded once again— like the two relationships that had come before him. Were there no good men left? I called a close friend of mine and retreated to her house for the night. Her husband was out of town on a business trip. For a while we sat together, drinking and despairing. All I could hear from her was how ruined I was now.

"What are you going to *do?*" she would ask me, like the idea of being single at forty-seven was worse than a death sentence. Inside, I felt my strength swell. I had raised Riley as a single mother. If I could do that, I could do anything. But here I was, my heart a mulch of colors swirled into a dark black abyss.

Being with Richard had stripped me of something. I felt broken and used up. I could not put my finger on the exact word for it yet. Jasmine offered to read my fortune and broke out the tarot cards. She meant well, but I needed to be alone. I retreated to the bathroom to soak away the events of that night.

As I rose to leave, she handed me a single card, which I carried to the bathroom. I filled the deep bath with hot water and steamed up every surface in the room. Once I had disappeared inside the heat, I reached for my glass of wine. Beneath it lay the card. I flipped it over lazily and saw the face staring back at me—it was Pan.

At first the image disturbed me. The half man half goat figure did not seem like a welcome sign. As the steam continued to rise, I relaxed and drifted into a light sleep. While dreaming, Pan danced on the card until a scene rose up in my mind's eye, vivid and intriguing. A new feeling emerged. I realized the Pan was not to be feared but embraced. There was a beauty to the scene. The Pan's age struck me as wondrous, and my heart opened wider.

Pan showed me that it was okay to love thy neighbor, to embrace liberation and the absence of rules. By my very nature, I would not kill. By my very nature, I would not steal. Without rules, living was simple. Spirituality was all that mattered. I could remove the noose around my neck whenever I wanted to.

I felt full of rage and joy; I danced, and sadness leaked from my body, draining the fear from me. I was one with the universe and everything inside it. I saw three graces ahead of me, and they embraced me with love. The dream was so intense that I woke smiling and crying.

It was purifying and animalistic. When I rose again, I felt better, cleansed by a wine-fueled dream. I sank back into the bath and heard flute music playing outside. Jasmine later told me that it was a song called "Debussy" by Syrnx. The Greek legend said that Syrnx was a woman in the forest that the god Pan was chasing.

She escaped him, so Pan became very sad. He picked up a reed and began playing it, which is how the flute was born. It was a long, mournful tune about the need to find the ideal mate. The music was so beautiful that Syrnx came back and they lay together. I reclined in the bath thinking about this visceral dream. I felt in my heart that it was a message.

Later that evening, when I googled the music Jasmine had been playing, I sat frozen to my chair. The composer had stated that he had been given the song by the god Pan, known as the god of the wild, of nature and rustic music, and of sexuality and revelry.

I knew what it meant right away. My heart had translated the dream into a clear message that I could no longer ignore. The word I had been searching for was "trapped." I had trapped my spirituality, limited my freedoms, and caged my personal growth for the men who I believed were meant to fulfill me.

I had sacrificed my artistic nature at the altar of finding my true mate. I knew that I had left the path. For all of my creativity and love, I had lost myself. And now the gods of the natural world were giving me a powerful message. I had to return home to the one place where I felt happiest—where I could run free, a woman without rules or limitations.

I had to move back to the Islands. There I could rekindle the fires that had once burned so bright inside me as a young child. I was terrified, but the sign was clear. With three failed relationships, I had fallen out of touch with myself. I needed to find my way back to happiness, the kind created by my spirit and not given to me by a man.

Leap of Faith

The idea stuck with me the next day and the next. It soothed my aching heart to know that I was being called home. That week I got to work packing up my life and leaving Richard to his. I had accumulated a lot of stuff over forty-seven years. As an artist, I had crates of unsold paintings, canvases, and art supplies.

With every move, I had to scale down. I was at it again, shedding my material possessions like they were the skin of an old life I did not want to take with me. I would touch down lightly on Maui soil for a fresh start. It was time to finally go after my long-held artistic dreams.

Riley, my son, was upset over the breakup and had to move his stuff out as well. Unlike me, he has never enjoyed accumulating things, not even books, much to my dismay. As a minimalist, his only prize possessions consisted of his iPhone, computer, gaming console, clothes, bass guitar, and some trophies and medals from his childhood.

I let go of a lot, believing that God and Mother Maui would guide me. What was left of my possessions was packed up and headed to a Matson ship that would travel for six weeks on the ocean before reaching Maui. I regretted having to split from my son, who would be going his own way now. It is never easy leaving behind a home that you have grown to love. Since the breakup, Riley had been home a lot more to help. Richard wanted me out in two weeks, but we compromised instead for another three months for my son to finish high school.

We were living a life of wealth in the East Bay, heading for an uncertain future. Riley would live with his father for a while before heading to the Air Force. Maui makes it easier for me to leave Richard, knowing that it is the right thing for me to do. In the meantime, I would move in with my sister Emily, who I have always been close with.

Emily drove all the way to Richard's house to help with the move, ever the protective older sister. In the space of one week, everyone I knew or loved had called me to express their grief over my situation. It was a hasty departure but one that was much needed when Richard's real nature became apparent.

Photos appeared on Facebook with him and a nice-looking blonde masseuse. I felt like he did this to humiliate me in front of everyone we knew after a seven-year relationship. Look at how quickly he cast me aside. Perhaps he had never truly loved me at all.

My sister is a nurse and commented, "Everyone seems to be on antidepressant drugs nowadays. You would be amazed how many people you interact with on a daily basis who are. I bet about half the population is." I didn't want to be part of the new "norm," so when my doctor tried to prescribe antidepressants, I refused and instead took up meditation and journaling. I prayed in earnest and cried a river. I exercised and drank in any and all inspiring, positive messages. I searched for signs of hope, and I started to watch comedy to make myself laugh again. Going through the stress of the move and major life changes while experiencing perimenopause made me lose sleep, and I needed my sleep desperately to function, so I started taking Ambien.

My friends and family were shocked about my decision to move to Maui, but they supported it. Then, two weeks before I was set to leave, I received another sign. I was contacted by the set designer from *Hawaii Five-0*. They bought seven of my original paintings for possible use on their set. Emily was thrilled and agreed that it was a sign. I mean, what are the chances that I would sell seven paintings bound for Hawaii with so many other artists online only a few weeks before I would be heading there myself? The timing was good, I would not have been able to sell them. They would have been on a ship with the rest of my belongings. It all happened in a whirlwind.

Friends and family met with me to say goodbye. Richard would pop in every other day to check on my progress. It took days to vacate that house! Then I was off to the Oakland airport with Riley, who was catching his flight to Seattle, Washington, to live with his father. Separating was harder on me than it was for him. He was at peace with everything that had happened—thank God.

Fresh out of high school and only nineteen years old, he enlisted with the Air Force and was placed on a waiting list for a job. The car felt heavy as I pulled into the airport. "I will park the car and walk you to the security line," I told him.

"Mom, don't bother. I will be fine. Besides, I don't want to see you cry and get all mushy in front of people," he said.

"Enjoy your time with your father. Please take care of yourself!"

The car shuddered to a halt on the curb, and we said our goodbyes in the car. "I love you, Riley. Call me as soon as you land so that I know you are okay," I said, tears welling in my eyes.

"I love you too, Mom, and I will." With that, he swung the door open and hopped out of the car. After strapping his backpack on, he unloaded his suitcases.

A hefty clunk, and the trunk was closed. One last wave, and he was off towards airport security. His dark brown hair was short, and he marched with confidence like he was already in the military, wheeling his two large suitcases behind him.

Tears fell freely now, and I stayed there for some time after he had left my sight. "Ma'am, please move on. You can't stay here," a security guard said to me, tapping on my window. I took a deep breath and pulled away, heading back to Danville to take care of business. I only had 24 hours to vacate my former family home.

During the wild process of organizing my son's stuff and dealing with the upheaval, I also managed to drive away from a gas station and rip the nozzle off the hose that was still connected to my gas tank. More insurance calls and a hefty credit card payment were added to the stress. It was a rough start. Even my cats cried the entire trip from Northern to Southern California. The sleeping medication I put in their food did not work. Behind my sunglasses, I shed tears about my misfortune and broken family life.

Along the way, Richard called me; he had clearly been crying. He wanted to tell me about things I left behind, but I told him that they were gifts. He broke down, selfishly casting guilt on me as I entertained his whimpering. We exchanged some strained words, and I told him not to call me again. I believe that was when I took the noose around my neck off.

Humble Beginnings

My recovery was officially underway, and I had a strong sense that I was on the right path. Glad to have Emily to lift my spirits during the long car ride, we arrived before sunset in a modest middle-class neighborhood. The homes there were simple single-story box houses as old as I was. Her home had four small bedrooms and one and a half bathrooms. We all had to share one shower.

I got my nephew's bedroom with a single bed and was grateful to have my own room. The house was filled with a family of five people, two yappy dogs, and one angry, fat cat that outright rejected my two cats and the prospect of sharing her home with them.

We crammed my possessions into an already jam-packed garage full of Emily's daughter's gear. Emily has two small dogs; Buffy is an affectionate old white dog, part Pomeranian, part Chihuahua, with light blue eyes and pink pupils. She reminded me of blind Master Po and often walked into furniture. Jackie was pure Pomeranian with auburn fur. By nature, she was a nervous little thing and growled when anyone got close to Emily and her bed at night.

My sister often thought Jackie's possessive behavior was amusing, although I found it unnerving—even more so when I saw that she allowed the dog to behave like this with her kids.

I discovered that my sister and I shared a t-shirt design with a little girl stick figure and stick dog both happy and in love. The slogan read, "Dogs make better boyfriends." We both put on our matching shirts, laughing, and took a photo. I prayed this would not be my future.

It struck me that I would be living there for three weeks before heading to Maui. It was so much smaller than Richard's house. As I often did during this dark time, I spiraled into bitter thoughts about Richard. That son of a bitch. This was all his fault. My thoughts bloomed into a fight with Emily from pure travel frustration, and I ended up crying on the curb that evening.

Even when Emily came over to apologize, I was still heavily upset. I could not understand what lesson in love I had not learned. Why did I keep choosing frogs? Where was my Prince Charming? Richard had swept me away at first. I thought he was the one.

Emily said, "You know, I can see why you fell for Richard. He did have some nice qualities. He was generous for one, but still, you did settle. He was a little toad."

"I guess he wasn't my Prince Charming in disguise after all," I said. "I have kissed too many frogs in my lifetime. I no longer want to meet any more amphibians, reptiles, or chameleons. I swear to God I'm done."

That night I only slept thanks to my constant companion, Ambien. I knew I had to get off the pills, but sleep was impossible without them. That needed to change. The next few days rolled by in a haze of emotion. It took time to realize what had happened to my life. Every evening I sat in Emily's backyard alone with my cats.

I thought about how I still loved Richard and worried about my future and my son's. Eventually, it would pass. Routines in Emily's house continued as normal in a blaze of busyness and habit. I was the outsider there, the new addition. People seemed to move around me in circles, leaving me to my thoughts and plans.

Spending time with my family took my thoughts off Richard for the most part. But in those quiet hours when I was alone, I would allow my mind to wonder who his new girlfriend was: the barista or the masseuse? It tormented me. In moments of weakness, I believed he had made a huge mistake.

Love and support surrounded me in Emily's home, and I rejoiced in it. They made sure that I was always included, and we went out often to take my mind off the aching solitude. When I was alone at home, I spent time organizing my virtual online business and began searching for places to stay on Maui.

Kauai is the most beautiful island in my opinion. Should I start there, island hop first, then move to Maui? It certainly would be a restorative location to start my journey, and boy, could I use some healing.

Inspired by my island memories, I wrote in my journal that night:

There are four frequented Hawaiian Islands, and they remind me of a family chain. Like four beautiful sisters who resemble one another, but are different and unique....

Kauai is a natural beauty who has aged well. She is an island to behold, with dramatic coastlines that leave me in a state of awe. Sometimes I feel the splendor is beyond this earthly realm and more like a fantasyland. When visiting the North Shore, I feel like I am on a movie set. The artist created a landscape that is surreal, and yet it is an earthbound, tangible place. God did some of his/her best creative work there.

She is lush with greenery and wears a jade-covered frock mixed with small patches of fiery red earth. Cascading blue and white tassel waterfalls adorn her like jewels. This island is beautiful with her tall, sheer green cliffs that fold like a pleated skirt into the ocean below. She is the oldest island in the chain and was born five million years ago. Her youthful fire is now extinct. The virgin black lava surface that she once was has decomposed over time and oxidized into rich red iron. She is petite in stature compared to her younger siblings in the chain of fire. Kauai is one of the wettest places on earth; it is what makes her so incredibly verdant.

With every visit to Kauai, I feel a strong mana (energy). I've felt it at Polihale State Park located on the Northwest Shores. The towering cliff face is round and worn by the environment. The dirt road leading to this beach is surrounded by tall grass and cane. You are away from it all. It is the road less traveled. I particularly notice this mana when I am strolling alone on one of the long sand beaches with turbulent surf scant of other human life. It is the energy radiating from the aina (land) and the kai (ocean). Consumed by nature's magnitude and force, I feel so small and yet connected.

The slower pace and beauty of Kauai I am particularly fond of. I wonder if I would get bored after too long. Are there enough jobs to support me if I had to find part-time work? The art galleries are slim, and I need to find a home for my art.

This would be a great island to heal and get away from it all...I find the locals friendly and spiritual energy high.

I continue to write...

Oahu is another beautiful island with similar terrain as Kauai. Her volcano is also extinct like her older sister. The topography appeals to me. I have a fondness for this place; it is where I fell in love as a small child. She nurtured me when I was a toddler, locking me into her embrace. You never forget your first love. This island will always have a special place in my heart for that reason alone.

Oahu has a cosmopolitan flare. She is vibrant, alive, there is much to do there. It would be easy to find work if I had to do so outside my online Maui vacation business. I would be near art galleries and the tourists, which would be important for my artist livelihood.

Waikiki's water is a captivating light blue during the day. I like that contrast against the soft white sand. The cityscape is enchanting in the evening, aglow with lights that reflect on the ocean and beckon one to play outdoors and participate in the action, the life, and entertainment. The city lights mesmerize and draw me in like a moth to a flame. The city is well maintained and clean.

The downside to Oahu is that she is too grown up and busy for my taste. A large metropolitan like her attracts crime and mega amounts of traffic. It would be like living on the mainland but better, of course, with beautiful scenery and weather year round.

On the shores of Waikiki, there is not much beach to stroll, parts washed away, and manmade narrow sidewalks connect the hotels. I like to run, so this is not ideal for me. I would have to hop, skip, and dance over people. It would disrupt my flow. In front of the luxury hotels, many tourists line the beach for part of the day, sitting or lying close together like sardines. How can one find solitude in this close proximity? I like to people watch, but to hear others' thoughts above my own is not my idea of peace.

I am particularly fond of Lanakai; this is next door to Kaneohe, where I grew up as a child on the Marine Corps base. However, the affordability factor is out of my reach.

The other beach towns are too close to a growing population of homeless and the beaches they occupy on the west side near Maili. You can drive for miles, and all you see are tents. This society is a mix of locals some with children; most have jobs but can't afford housing. Here they reside with people who have been left behind by the system or have deeper troubles, like mental illness or drug problems. People come here on their own to drop out in paradise in the hopes that the land will be less harsh and the elements gentler. With a denser population, the locals do not seem as friendly, and they are not so trusting. I decide to pass. I did not remember feeling that spiritual vibe I was looking for.

Then there is Maui, the third sister, who I will save for last...

The island of Hawaii, the baby sister; her nickname is the Big Island because she is the largest of them all. She is also the youngest, and her tender age is more than half a million years old. She is immature and erupts off and on over her youthful lifespan. She is the one known to have a hot temper. In 1983 she erupted again, experiencing new growing pains. Kilauea is the most active volcano in the world with the longest historical flow ever recorded. She continues to grow physically, her land mass slowly expanding.

The goddess of fire is named Pele; she is alive and well and resides in the heart of Kilauea. She is the earth-eating spirit who is both creator and destroyer. Legend says if you remove her volcanic rock, she will put a curse on you.

Dolphins visit the Captain Cook area and swim with humans in the open ocean. I swam with a pod of dolphins once; they were just as curious about me as I was about them. I will never forget their communication—whistling and clicking—I felt at one with them.

When leaving the Kona airport, all you see is black lava rock that stretches for miles along the highway. It feels barren, and sometimes you can smell a hint of sulfur. The lava fields are a stark contrast against the distant blue ocean. Kailua-Kona downtown sits on the ocean front. It is charming. There are many casual open air dining establishments along the water's edge. The homes are more affordable here compared to the sister islands, especially the closer you get to the active volcano and vog.

This side of the island, Kailua-Kona is the dry side and a safe distance from the goddess Pele. Many of the restaurants adorn lights to create a tropical, festive mood in time for sunset hour. Instruments strum to the beat of the surf gently lapping the shore, and performers sing an enchanting Hawaiian melody accompanying a lone, graceful hula dancer swaying her hips and wearing a soft smile. She gestures with her hands, telling a Hawaiian story. I love the vibe of that town. If I decided to live on the Big Island, I would prefer it there.

I've stayed on the east side, Puna district. My friends needed me to housesit and manage their vacation rental business for two weeks. My temporary residence was their two-story octagon shape home, a short car ride to downtown Pahoa.

Pahoa is a historic town that has a handful of clothing stores and gift shops and three dining establishments. My favorite was Luquins Mexican restaurant! The small community made me feel like I was living in the Wild West. Twenty miles north of Pahoa is a larger city Hilo. Visiting both cities feel like a stroll back in time.

Mauna Kea and Mauna Loa stop traveling clouds off the Pacific and tap the precious resource of rain. This creates the lush foliage and underground water tables for the island. The rain works to break down the lava rock into rich soil, and with the help of the pounding ocean surf, sandy beaches form. It is an untamed Eden. The beaches are still in their infancy. The long, wide sandy beaches are not as plentiful here.

I will never forget our family visit to the top of Mauna Kea, the tallest sea mountain in the world. I felt one with heaven; never had I seen so many stars glitter and dance upon the night sky. How can earth possibly be the only planet to sustain life in such a big galaxy of light?

I don't know if living this close to an active volcano is a good idea.

Too much isolation for long feels lonely for a social person like me. I need a happy medium. A healthy amount of solitude and the right mix of energy and camaraderie with my fellow human beings. I prefer charming small towns compared to busy bustling cities...Maui is the place for me.

As I typed these words on my laptop, I switched over to Google and searched for places to stay on Maui. I came across a couple named Rama and Sita, who owned the Lotus Retreat and Farm. The pitch on the website caught my attention: "A place for mature souls," it read. Unlike many other places on the island, this was a deeply spiritual area. I knew instantly it was the best place for me.

I desperately needed to be reminded that I had something truly great to look forward to. If I watched enough of these positive programs on spirituality with guests from Maui, it might take me out of my funk.

I came across several YouTube videos about this couple and their Lotus Retreat. The interview that spoke to my heart was "Paradise Found Awaken Your Creative Soul"—Sita, Maui Hawaii by Lucia Macari the Luscious Life Tour.

At once, I was captivated by a rhythmic chant; it was Sita's beautiful Hawaiian melody, her feminine voice strong, steady, and poignant. The side of a pahu (drum) was beaten softly and in unison with her song, creating a pulse that was reminiscent of a heartbeat: tick tock tick, tick tock, tick, tick tock.

I was transported to a tropical destination in Haiku, Maui, deep in the forest to a spiritual retreat that sits on towering emerald cliffs overlooking the Pacific Ocean. We were led down a driveway and to an entrance lined with large gray rocks that hold back flourishing vegetation from treading forward on a red walkway. Inviting colors of purple and green tea leaves intermingle with wispy greenery sprinkled with dainty pink, white, and yellow flowers.

What a nice, welcome home bouquet. I can almost smell the flora! I thought while watching. The camera revealed even more and took me beyond the path to a bright green lawn with waving coconut trees and sparkling, distant seas. Slowly, we were led to the cinnamon-color Bamboo Malu home; it looked inviting and warm. There were solar panels to catch the sun's energy and a water catchment system for the ponds. This community guest house is where I would eventually begin my stay; I would take daily strolls here in the near future.

The scene shifts to the interior of a home. Lucia and her guest, Sita, sit on a couch filled with red fluffy pillows. There are two large windows behind them that let in the green landscape. The beauty and serenity drew me in as much as the rhythmic Hawaiian chant. Sita is a beautiful mature woman. Her long auburn hair cascades over her breasts. She is dressed in a sheer gold leopard skin print dress that hangs comfortably on her tall, slender figure. She has a lovely face and a regal presence. Lucia is attractive too; and looks to be in her late twenties with chin-length, silky black hair. She wears a white plumeria tucked behind her left ear.

With microphone in hand, Lucia begins the interview in her Italian accent. She has the enthusiasm of an inquisitive child: "Heeeloh my delicious co-creators. Lucia here on the beautiful island of Maui, Hawaii, with scrumptious Sita...thank you for hosting me on this gorgeous property. It is very nurturing.... We are all the way up north on Maui next to Haiku." She lifts her free hand to the universe. "Really, how do you call this place?"

Sita smiles and her deep blue eyes sparkle as she turns to look at the camera and speaks in her Austrian accent: "It's the area of Huelo, and we are on the North Shore right where the sun rises, where the day begins. Most visitors who come to Maui stay where the sun descends, but we are where the morning light first appears...."

I usually stay where the sun sets myself. I should experience more of the sunrise...how symbolic to start each day this way with new hope, new beginnings, rebirth, witnessing heavenly rays slowly color the earth, when all is quiet and peaceful, when the air is cool and comfortable. The only sounds to break the silence, the ocean and morning birds' chorus. Starting my day at dawn is probably the best time to commune with God before the chatter of the day takes over... I thought to myself.

Lucia continues, "This is a very, very special spot. The mana here is really pure and superb; I want to acknowledge you for that. Because you had a big dream...you have done so many things. You have been a tantric teacher for over 25 years, and you wrote a scrumptious book that is coming out soon—and you have record labels. Tell us, when did you decide to make the move and respond to the message of your heart to make this vision a reality? I mean, this is like out of thin air. You are the queen of manifestation."

I was mesmerized; she had my attention. I needed to know more. I wanted to stay at this place to resuscitate my depleted soul and jumpstart my heart. I needed a miracle, some guidance—to be surrounded by pristine nature and the positive energy of this home in the jungle. I was sure it would mend this broken heart of mine quickly. I continued to listen:

"Mahalo, Lucia. The message your heart receives can come to you at any time of your life, and in my life, mine came very early in my twenties. Growing up in Austria, my intuition spoke loud and clear and led me to India, where I found spiritual masters. They really, really inspired me, and I got excited to know more about mysticism...in 1987 I came to this land and created this organic farm and retreat for people to come to heal and rest—a spiritual artistic community..."

Okay, this woman Sita is speaking my language. Wow! An artistic community! Spirituality and mysticism. During my busy, working, materialistic, responsible planned life and demands of being a single mother and provider, I lost touch with this part of myself—at least some of the philosophies of tuning into the universe on a regular basis to ground myself and to live in awe, appreciation, and wonderment of what life really means. I did not carve out time for commune with Source. To be still, quiet, reflective. I really missed that inner connection. I longed to tap into this buried side of myself. I must be in a place with likeminded individuals, I feel a connection already to Sita and her Lotus Retreat.

Sita continued, "...I went to India...there was that calling...and when I went into the temple and for the first time saw the union of man and woman and saw that sexuality was part of some of their spiritual teachings, that really spoke to me because that was the missing piece I couldn't get in our traditional Christian upbringing—that sexuality is sacred—and that really sparked me. I had to know what is this to embody your spiritualty, not just from here up," (as she places her hand below her breast and raises her hand towards her face).

"It is really living it. Living luscious... Finding that wisdom within, owning it, and embodying it, that is really what is important.... It starts with altering your thoughts, knowing that sexuality is beautiful and sanctified sexuality is sacred and intimacy and sexuality is part of our birthright. We have to learn it, develop it, and not just do it and not know what we are doing.

"It starts at a young age. We need to give people the right

education about how to nurture their sensual energy, and then you can bring that power into your consciousness, and that is really the path of awakening...and of course there are many conduits.... I can only say that is the passageway that leads to the heart, your transformation station for sexual energy or a guiding and creative force used to manifest.

"If your emotional heart is not a part of creating it, it's not going anywhere.... It is your heart that needs to be accessible, to be tender and kind...there is not one power or sexual energy; it is all merged. Do you make use of your sensual energy in an honored practice? Using it with tantric and breathing practices, awareness, and meditation, and, of course, you need a loving partner—one who you can really bond with...seeing the divine in each other and in everything, this really opens the heart."

What is tantra? I had never heard the term before. It all sounded so sexual.... I would be interested to explore this as long as it is not some weird hippy, swap love partners, or groupie thing. Then again, she made it sound so beautiful. She did say it is best to do tantra with a loving partner, one that I can personally bond with.

Now to find the right partner. I don't want to search for a relationship when I move to Maui. I don't want to do any online dating. I want to find love organically. Be led to the right man, the right people, go with the flow. Let the Maui Magic work, let go of control...put any fears aside and trust in God and the Universe to provide and lead.

The interview continued with Sita: "Mother Earth is the temple that my temple is built upon. Temple is a translation of treating things with sacredness, with consciousness, with kindness, and if I can treat my own body with that love, there is no separation; we are all connected.... My home I want to treat like a temple.... Every room here at the Lotus Retreat has a small altar of reference to remind our visitors that everything is sacred. It is the consciousness that we belong together.... We are interconnected as brothers and sisters."

This place sounds so cool! I had a soft smile on my face as I remembered the feelings and truths she spoke about the connectedness to Mother Earth. *I needed to reawaken that part of me that was shut down, temporarily asleep. I needed to find the misplaced key to unlock that door, to reach the other side. Perhaps if I stayed there first, for one month or ninety days, I could get my bearings and heal, quickening my return to oneness, bliss, true love, and happiness.*

Sita expressed her wishes: "We all deserve to live in paradise. ...I'm grateful for all the teachers I had, and we want to share our wisdom with our guests. I hope you get a chance to talk to my husband Rama about his music. It is another form of communication that makes life luscious...."

Lucia asked, "You took your vision from the imaginary to the real. Did you tap into the invisible realm of spirit, deities, angels, the Universe...did you really call for Mother Earth for assistance?"

"Lucia, I'm just a vessel for God. We all are if we allow the holy spirit to move us.... I have learned it from Rama, to listen to your heart sincerely if you take a moment, be in the present, and you place your hand on your heart and simply listen. Pay attention to what moves you and what gift you want to leave, and what really makes you happy there can only be good. This is luscious living. There can only be love...." (She shook her head, teared up, and became speechless.)

Lucia turned away, looked into the camera with her dark brown eyes sparkling, and became her animated self with a radiant smile: "Luscious, luscious, my wonderful co creators, I told you, bellissimo, bellissimo, there it is all these wonderful stories from around the planet. I'm so grateful to be sitting here. Thank you for manifesting this magical place for mature, creative souls to come and rest. Thank you."

"Mahalo for being here, Lucia, and I would love for whoever

sees this video to come. I'm really touched, and I know that spirit is working in all of us. Aloha."

Synchronicity is at work because Sita must know energetically that I will be calling her soon.

Lucia ended the program: "Aloha, my beautiful co-creators, we send you tremendous love and magnificent mana from this power spot." (She laughed, and the two beautiful goddesses waved at the camera.) *This tantra sounds like a harnessing of your sexual energy, and the idea sounds similar to a classic book I read, a favorite,* Think and Grow Rich *by Napoleon Hill, published in 1937.*

"The Mystery of Sex Transmutation"

The desire for sexual expression is natural and inborn in us. It cannot be submerged or removed; instead, it should be given an outlet through various forms of expression.

The mind responds to stimuli and high vibration rates. These are known as "intense desire," "creative imagination," and "enthusiasm." The mind also responds to stimulation; the most powerful of these is the urge to have sex. When this power is channeled, it can lift men into a higher sphere of thought, which allows them to master their anxieties and get over minor annoyances, which keep them stuck on the lesser spiritual plane...misunderstanding and misusing this powerful force so that they are only able to achieve the status of lower animals. Overindulgence in sexual expression can also be negative; it can become a habit that is enormously detrimental to creative efforts, just as much as alcohol and narcotics can be.

Remove the idea that loves only happens once. It comes and goes, sometimes without reason—but no two love experiences are the same. The biggest difference of them all is that sex is biological, while love is spiritual. Love on its own cannot bring about happiness in a marriage, and neither can sex when it stands alone. But when these two emotions are entwined, marriage can cause a state of mind closest to the spiritual that you will ever know.

Taking the Plunge

We never know how our prayers will be answered. I was sold on the inspiration of the land, this power spot for creative types—to be in a place where Mother Earth nurtures her children, providing us with her medicinal healing balm and her sweet rainbow nectar to the thirsty souls who visit.

This is the Maui Magic I wanted to experience. I would start my journey there and figure out the details of where to move next. This was the most spontaneous I had been in a long time. I felt hopeful and inspired to take this leap of faith, trusting in God and in the Universe to catch me as I freefall and gently land upon a billowy field of Maui green overlooking Huelo and the Pacific Ocean.

I booked a one-way ticket to Maui and accommodation at the Lotus Retreat and Farm with Rama and Sita. They seemed like the free-spirited types I needed to be around. The day came when I had to leave for my Maui adventure. I was hopelessly nervous and excited beyond words. A new adventure, done alone, and done just for me. This was the beginning!

Maui would breathe new life into me; I just knew it. I was a pioneer striking out into a new world. With some savings that I had accrued, I was on my way. Somehow I would make it happen for myself. I said my goodbyes to my family and left for the airport in a taxicab.

I decided to swear off sex for a while so that I could focus on my self-discovery. Sex just complicated things, and if I happened to meet the right man on Maui, he would wait for me. The next time I made love, it would be on my honeymoon with a real man, not a Richard, not a Nathan, and not a Sam.

The taxicab pulled to the curb, confidence oozing from every pore. No man could hold me back! No man could keep me down! I was a free woman on a mission. I marveled at my independence as I stood in the airport security line, and I lifted bags onto the security belt as it ran through the x-ray machine.

In the lane next to me, I noticed an Indian woman my own age doing the same thing. I smiled at her and she at me. As I was being allowed through the security check, I noticed they had stopped to search her bag. "What is this?" demanded a young security screener. "Ma'am, what is this device?" he said again, causing a scene.

I glanced back at the woman, who was positively beaming. In the security guard's hand was a long pink vibrator, which he was waving from left to right—examining it from all angles. I could see that she was embarrassed but proud. Again the security screener demanded an answer as rampant giggles broke out behind her in the queue.

"Honey, if I have to tell you what that thing is, we have a problem," she said. I watched as the young security screener's face turned red as it dawned on him.

As I walked away, a voice came from behind the Indian lady. A black woman said, "Right on, sister. You tell him it's none of his business!"

I saw a handsome airline pilot come up to her, and he said, "I like the way you handled yourself back there. Here is my card. Call me..."

With my mind on the pink vibrator, I found myself laughing. After passing through security, I visited the airport bar to wait for my boarding call.

"A cosmopolitan," I said to the barman as I sat down to rest my aching feet. My choice of shoes for the plane ride had not been the most practical, although they did make me feel sexy. It was loud and bustling as airport bars are, and people came and went at will. I took a long sip of a delicious Cosmo and settled into the wait, my thoughts on Maui.

"Hello," came a voice behind me. A tall man with dark brown hair flecked with grey settled next to me at the bar.

"Hi," I said politely, keeping to myself.

"Nice shoes," he said, smiling broadly.

I could not help but notice how handsome he was. Dressed in a crisp grey suit with a black tie, he smelled like oak polish and herbal soap.

I shot him another offish smile and continued with my drink. "Are you going to drink that?" he persisted.

"Most definitely."

"How about another one? Would you drink that?" he pressed, his hazel eyes glinting in the airport light.

"Quite persistent, aren't you?" I said, turning towards the man.

"Only when I see a conversation worth having."

"Oh?" I asked him. "And what makes you think I'm the right woman for that?"

He gestured towards the barman, who settled two new drinks on the countertop. "Your shoes. I haven't seen an original pair of red heeled Louboutin's in some years."

"You know your shoes," I admitted. they had been a gift from that cheating bastard Richard.

"I do, though I must say you wear them well. I'm Thomas," he added, holding out his hand. I shook it politely. It was soft and warm.

"Katie," I offered, "and thank you for the compliment."

He inclined his head and drank whiskey from his glass. I felt compelled to continue the conversation, although I knew it was a pick-up tactic already.

There was something wonderfully appealing about this man. "So are you a shoe salesman?"

"Of sorts. I buy fashion accessories for a global distributor based in Japan. I'm heading there now. It's a very rewarding job."

"I'll bet," I said, feeling the urge to flirt blossom inside me.

"It's not like that. But it has been a long while since I met someone like you."

My cheeks turned pink, like the vibrator the security screener had discovered earlier. I giggled into my Cosmo.

"Where are you heading?"

"Maui. I am moving there, but I can't tell you why."

"You can. I have at least five minutes until my flight boards." His eyes bore into mine.

I took a breath. "I am going on a spiritual retreat to rediscover myself as an artist and writer."

"Ah there, you see, I knew you would be a fascinating woman to talk to. I write a little myself, though nothing I will ever publish. Just personal insight, that kind of thing."

I drained my second drink and crossed my legs. "I'm working on a book," I decided then and there, "about moving on after someone has trampled your heart."

A tone sounded in the background like a distant alarm. Thomas rose, paused for a moment, and took out his wallet. He withdrew a neat grey card with his contact details emblazoned on the front. "I would love to hear all about it. I've just left a bad relationship myself. I hope this is not too forward, but here is my card. I would like to stay in touch. Please email or call sometime."

I took his card, said goodbye, and watched as he pulled his neat carry-on bag behind him. My heart thudded in my chest. *What are the chances of that?* I thought. *Meeting such a handsome man in the airport right before I leave forever!* Was my life just a succession of ironic experiences? Sometimes I thought so.

I pocketed the card and rose twenty minutes later to board my flight to Maui—feeling extra confident in my recognizably fashionable heels. He knew how to make a woman feel desired, that one. Good thing he was gone! The flight to Maui was not like others I had taken in my life. I was filled with feelings of anxiety and loss once I had settled down.

I still did not know where I would rent a place to live. I could not afford to stay in the condo I owned; I needed the rental income. I still did not know if I would visit the other Hawaiian Islands. All I knew was that I was heading to Maui for three months first and staying on at the Lotus Retreat. There I would have to make some big decisions, all the while writing my first book and healing a broken heart.

The idea to write a book had occurred to me before, although now it seemed like the logical thing to do. I had only realized it, of course, talking to handsome Thomas at the bar. From the moment I arrived on Maui I would keep a journal of my experiences, tracking every experience from start to finish.

The longer I thought about it, the stronger the idea became in my mind. I would write a book about being a woman alone on a journey, about soul searching and trying out every spiritual method of expanding my consciousness and understanding. I would take my readers with me on a one-way adventure into the unknown world of self-discovery.

This was my destiny in the art capital of Hawaii.

Chapter 3

The Lotus Retreat

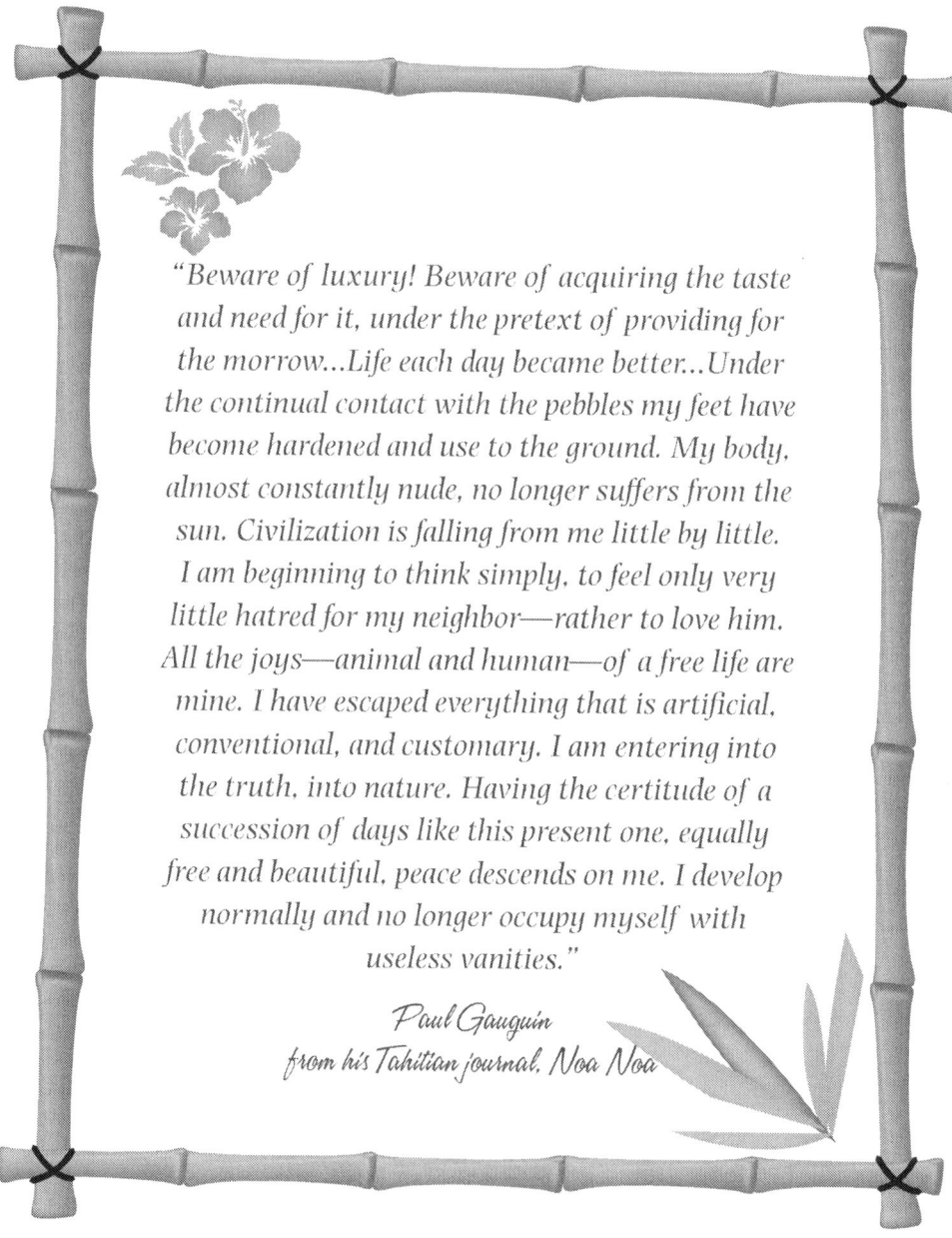

"Beware of luxury! Beware of acquiring the taste
and need for it, under the pretext of providing for
the morrow...Life each day became better...Under
the continual contact with the pebbles my feet have
become hardened and use to the ground. My body,
almost constantly nude, no longer suffers from the
sun. Civilization is falling from me little by little.
I am beginning to think simply, to feel only very
little hatred for my neighbor—rather to love him.
All the joys—animal and human—of a free life are
mine. I have escaped everything that is artificial,
conventional, and customary. I am entering into
the truth, into nature. Having the certitude of a
succession of days like this present one, equally
free and beautiful, peace descends on me. I develop
normally and no longer occupy myself with
useless vanities."

Paul Gauguin
from his Tahitian journal, Noa Noa

The Day of Arrival

Men. Men, men, men, men, men. Sometimes it feels like my whole life has been about them. The longer I sat in my seat on the plane, the more resolute I became. The experience at the Lotus Retreat would not be about men. I had to dig deep and not dissolve into a love-struck mess every time a man gave me attention.

I was my own woman now and free to explore my creative side without restraint. I had to learn to put my obsession with finding the perfect, healthy relationship aside. My art, my book, myself—I needed to remember these. Even as I sat there, I heard my mother's voice echoing in my head. She would disapprove of where I was headed. The Lotus Retreat and Farm was full of hippies, in her opinion.

They thought I was being brave. My mother reminded me to not become a lazy hippy. My father told me I would need to collect cans to support myself if I decided to be a full-time artist. Spending three months in the jungle with a bunch of strangers—it sounded so cool when I first did my research. I told them I would be okay, and I would be. It was only three months. I had to remind everyone about the positive parts of the YouTube video to convince myself I had made the right decision. After all, it was too late now. I had already paid them three months' advance rent, and there was no refund. My mother's voice echoed in my memory: "Katie, don't drink the Kool-Aid." That was a good start.

I was hoping for a place where I could finally find some peace and introspection, where I could get off the sleeping pills and collapse into my creative spirit. Maui was the art capital of Hawaii, and I would establish my vacation rental business there; it was easier to check on the properties. I could take the time to plan what to do next; maybe I should try smoking marijuana, the medical approved kind, and do some serious soul searching. As the airplane doors opened, the cabin was filled with a familiar tropical breeze. The air was sweeter here. As I left the plane behind, the sunshine cascaded over the gleaming airport.

I inhaled that refreshing Aloha spirit as I waited for my baggage to spiral towards me. The airport here was different. Passengers wore tank tops, shorts, flip flops, and vibrant hula shirts. There was nothing sexier than a tanned man in a Hawaiian hula shirt! Suddenly I was surrounded by them. I had forgotten how sexually charged it was on this electric island.

I picked up my rental car and lugged my four heavy bags from the luggage cart into the trunk. I worked up a sweat. Richard usually handled all the heavy lifting. Now there was only me to take care of business. The gentle breeze encircled me as I pulled out of the small airport parking lot. I was away! I was here! I was... what was I doing?

I veered off the side of the road, my hands clutching the steering wheel of my tiny blueberry, box-shaped economy vehicle. I realized all at once what I had done. Had I gone insane? I was alone! I could barely lift my bags into the trunk! How was I going to survive living here on my own? Doubts swirled around my head, and I had to take a moment to reorient.

I looked at myself squarely in the rearview mirror. *"Katie, hey!*

Snap out of it. This is the right decision. You are here already, and you are going to make the best of it. It's supposed to be scary! It's supposed to be challenging! You belong here. Forget what Mom said. Forget Richard. This is about you! You! Get it together!"

As I pointed angrily at myself, a family of five drove by, and the youngest son shook his hand, sharing a shaka sign, reminding me to hang loose. I smiled and returned the greeting. After all, I was right. A little overwhelmed, but right. I just needed to find my way to the Lotus Retreat. I said a silent prayer, rolled my window all the way down to allow the island breeze to embrace me, and set off—leaving my panic behind.

I drove to South Kihei to check on my vacation rental and stopped in next door to my favorite sandwich shop, 808 Deli. Starved from the plane ride, I ordered a chicken salad sandwich and devoured it in the car as I sped off on the traffic-free road to the Lotus Retreat. I only had another hour before check-in, and I was running late.

I drove past many open air restaurants and saw Mount Haleakala, the dormant volcano, in the distance. It is a patchwork of greens and brown oxidized iron soils. The beaches were gorgeous, and the sandwich was delicious. Good food always puts my mind at ease. I was crazy to be here, but Emily always said, "Alone or with a man, it's always best to be the crazy one."

Home Is Where the Heart Is

I pulled out the directions I kept folded on a printed piece of paper and began the journey off the beaten track to the Lotus Retreat and Farm.

The sun was setting, casting a pretty glow upon the sky. The road leading to Haiku was a two-lane highway that hugged the coastline. The farther I traveled, the more twists and turns there were in the road. It was the beginning route to the Road to Hana.

After ten minutes of driving, the landscape changed from quaint buildings and shanty shacks to lush greenery and rolling hills tinted a warm orange glow. What homes there are out there were mostly obscured by foliage.

The drive was beautiful. So far so good—written directions were guiding me correctly. My cell phone stopped working when I passed the cemetery. Another fifteen minutes passed, and I come to a sharp turn in the road and passed mile marker three. I slowed down as instructed; my turn off was coming up. I saw a crudely built green sheltered area with a bench. I wondered if it was a bus stop. There were several rows of mail boxes that lined the corner. This was where I needed to turn.

The corner was sharp, and to cross over, I had to be careful for oncoming traffic and watch for cars that might be riding my tail. Luckily, the roads are never really congested here. I crossed over the two-lane highway and pulled into THE DOOR OF FAITH Church Road. One needs faith just to cross the two lanes and even more faith to continue on the partially paved lane that eventually turns into narrow dirt roads filled with pot holes. I wove to avoid them. The deeper I traveled on this road, it became muddy with more holes and rocks scattered about. I missed my blue Mercedes; the blueberry sedan I was driving enhanced every stone and twig in the road.

It followed on a sharp incline along a narrow dirt road, fitting only one small car at a time. "It's the middle of the jungle here," I said to myself, turning down the radio and pushing my chicken sandwich wrappers aside. There it was, the entrance. I recognized it instantly from the online photos and videos.

Tibetan prayer flags hung from the pole over the golden amber bamboo fence that sat behind a dark brown octagon gazebo, also made of bamboo. "Aptly named," I mused, craning my neck and pulling into a parking space. Inside the gazebo was Saraswati, an

Indian deity. The videos online said that all people with artistic expression were welcome here and that the goddess of creativity was there to inspire all.

I winked at her, knowing that she may be the reason I get my book finished. A red pathway with large stones held back bushels of flora with broad green and purple ti leaves, believed to ward off evil spirits. The colorful path took me all the way to the Bamboo Malu House, a four-bedroom home with two bedrooms downstairs and two upstairs. The guests shared the main house together.

I had booked the Indian Room, a place with lots of light and endless views of the ocean, the Haleakala Crater, and the jungle. I was eager to see it in person. As I moved up the path and inside the door, I spotted a few people milling about the house. They headed into a large back room where I read Rama and Sita host their classes.

As I stood waiting for someone to approach me, I checked my phone. Oh no, no signal! I resigned myself to the idea that no outside contact by phone would be therapeutic. After five minutes I noticed a tattered sign stuck to the door with Scotch tape that read, "For late arrivals, please call Rama's cell phone." Great.

I decided to act. "Is anyone here?" I called.

A few moments later I was approached by two women—one older, closer to my age, with thick blonde hair and bright blue eyes, and the other younger, in her late twenties, with blonde hair down to her waist and a deep olive tan. "You must be our new guest, Katie!" said the fairer of the two. "I am Crystal, and this is Aria. We'll get a hold of Rama for you."

I stood awkwardly holding my carry-on bag as Crystal disappeared into another room. Aria was still smiling at me, and I felt compelled to talk. "So do you work with Rama?"

"We are the Woofers around here," she mentioned, dreamily scratching her arm.

"A Woofer?" I asked, confused.

"Oh, yes, think of us as farm interns, willing Workers on Organic Farms, WOOF for short; we trade work to live here and learn about organic farming."

"Wow, that's interesting," I said, wishing I had a pen in my hand to jot down some notes. "How does that work?"

"We work about four hours a day, then the rest of the time we get to ourselves. There are five of us right now: Crystal, me, Alex, Michael, and Josh. You'll meet them soon, I'm sure."

Crystal returned with Rama, who was six feet of wild black hair and dark brown recessed eyes in a skinny, pale frame. He seemed a little slow and dazed at first, but this suited the yoga pants and white flowing shirt he was wearing. He was straight out of a hippy drum circle.

The moment Rama spoke, I liked him. His deep baritone voice washed over me. "Katie! Glad you made it out here in one piece! We expected you a little earlier. Follow me." He led me to the Indian room, and it was everything I expected it to be, although it smelled like herbal essence.

"A few things as you settle in. This is sacred land because we are right next to Huelo, which is a vortex spot of great energy. If you want, you can make your way over to the Hanehoi waterfall, where the energy is strongest. Watch out for the aliens though. Every now and then we get a UFO wandering over the property, so keep your eyes peeled."

I laughed but quickly cut it short when I realized he was deadly serious. "Here is everything you need," he added, handing me a map of the property while looking nervously around the ceiling— as if at any moment we might be accosted by little green men. There was a clearly marked waterfall on the map along with the two meditating temples. The beach was about a thirty-minute hike. After signing a waiver that he hastily produced, I was ready to settle in.

"Oh, and there is only one bathroom here, as you know from the website. You may want to visit it before I give you your heart reading, if you want it." Confused, I followed Rama's gesture to the back of my jeans...a wet slab of lettuce was pasted to my rear thigh. "Don't worry about it, man," he said. "You should enjoy what you eat, no matter where it ends up."

Mortified, I nipped off to the communal bathroom to clean up before heading back into the kitchen for my heart reading. I was excited to hear what Rama had to say about me. I settled into a wooden chair next to the counter. As I sat down, some young men waved to me from behind a sliding door. People were very friendly here.

I heard my mother's voice in my mind again. "Now you done it, Katie. You have joined a cult, and they will want you to do sex things with them!" I hoped that was not the case. At the same time, I could not help noticing how handsome the young men were. Good thing I changed out of my Louboutins on the plane.

Rama sat across from me and skidded his chair over until he was right up close. "Okay, do you mind if I put my hand on your skin, on top of your heart? It's not a sexual thing." I can't explain why, but I trusted him. Here was a strange man that I had met only minutes before, and I was allowing him to touch me. Should I be concerned?

I pushed the thought from my mind and nodded. His hand was big and warm, and we breathed together in unison. "Please gaze into my eyes," he added, becoming very serious. For a few awkward minutes, all he did was look at me. Each time I wanted to speak, he shushed me. Then he spoke again.

"Whoa, shit, man, you have a lot of stuff going on here...you have been through a lot recently too." Now it was my turn to be tongue tied. I nodded, and my eyes watered. "You are here to write your book about this place and your experience here," he continued. "All your life you have nurtured other people. It is time for you to do the same for yourself. You have a good heart. You will have fun here, I promise you that."

Rama pulled his hand away, and I felt connected to him somehow. I knew the healing had begun. In all my years, I had never felt an emotional release like that—had I been so lacking in acknowledgement of myself that I was starved of real connection?

"This reminds me of my birth in a lot of ways," he said, standing up.

"Your birth?" I said, rising too.

"Yeah, Dr. Mason was going to abort me; he didn't think my mother would survive childbirth. Then two nuns and a security guard stopped him and said, 'We do not do abortions here. You must disengage the clamps and leave.' Then Dr. Johnson took over."

"Dr. Johnson was an intuitive; he delivered me. I remember the day like it was yesterday. Sometimes I wake up and still feel like the clamps are around my head.... My mother's daily prayers and love kept me alive." He wandered off, leaving me to my thoughts. I came to understand that Rama had many strange stories to share. It was part of his ethereal charm.

I met one of the paying guests that evening, a nice man named Forest, who was heading back from the waterfall to his bedroom, and Shiva, the yoga teacher who lived on the property. The house was fairly empty that first night. I took time to begin my journals in the Indian room. There was no cell signal or Wi-Fi or anything that could distract. It was just me and the pattering rain outside. I began to write:

Rama explained to me that he has been doing heart readings for over thirty years. He takes the time to connect by placing his hand on a person's heart, flesh to flesh; it is like touching

God. He allows his awareness to expand to really feel the heart vibrationally; our bodies are made up of mostly water. He starts feeling the heart; he actually says hello to the heart and then listens for the heart to say hello back. He takes what he gets—what attitude, state of mind that he "feels"—and takes whatever answer he gets, whatever emotions from the heart, and he sees pictures from the past, present, and future. Some readings can be so overpowering with love sometimes like a symphony coming at him.

That night I took a sleeping pill, and locked my bedroom door; it was my first evening in a strange place.

My First Full Day at the Retreat

I woke with the clattering of rain and leaves against the tin roof, a chorus of white noise. Palm trees rustled next to my window, and I could smell salt in the air from the nearby ocean. Low voices murmured outside as a rooster crowed in the distance. My first day in paradise.

My bedroom was directly above the kitchen, so by 7 a.m. heavenly smells were filtering in under my closed door. Groggy, I rose and grabbed the bag that contained my towel, soap, and other toiletries. As I made my way to the bathroom, I noticed a table that stood in the hallway. Upon the table was a deck of cards— "Take one a day," said the label, so I did.

Only one word was on my card that day— "courage" —I guessed I would need a lot of it to get through the next few months alone here. As I showered, I realized that there was very little privacy in the house; three people knocked on my door at different times. As I stood under the hot water, I reviewed the decisions that had brought me to this place.

I knew I was fine financially for the next three months, but soon

I would need to earn more money to get by. With two houses to maintain, one on the mainland and another here on Maui, and some debt, I still had to find an affordable home to rent. But enough of that for now; I had to at least try to enjoy my first day at the retreat.

I was meeting Rama downstairs for an early morning music class. I dressed hastily tying my hair into a bun and applied some lip gloss to my lips. I chose comfortable clothes and walked barefoot, no shoes allowed indoors. There was a general bustle in the house as I walked past the kitchen towards the music room. Rama sat there with a few other house guests; they were all in the meditation pose.

He strummed gently on a guitar and spoke. "You will discover that everything that you have ever created first began with a sound. This room is here because someone had a sound inside their head that said, 'I think we should build a building here.' If you want to know the substance of anything, you don't need to look at it, man. Looking at it, all you'll see is form. If you want to know the substance of something, you listen to it."

"Listen to the wind, and you will know it. This is the root of all manifestation. Sound is the most substantial thing that we know of in the universe." I joined the group and sat cross-legged, listening to Rama's lecture. "Scientists have discovered the whole universe is based on one note. It turned out to be B flat, but check this out—when I'm sitting with a woman and we are playing music together, the heat will rise from the both of us. We will vibrate at the same time, and this invokes sexual energy. Eventually, I become so connected to her that I can read her mind!"

"It's not the form of the music that heals; it's the state the musician is in while making the music that does the healing. Can you dig it? If I played a recording of the Dalai Lama meditating right now, you wouldn't hear a thing, but the mood in the room would change.

"You can also start with visual stimuli. I'll imagine that I'm in a hot tub with naked girls, and suddenly the music comes. Have happy thoughts...composing music always comes from an experience, usually love. If you want to write music, go back to that...love, I mean. Lots of cultures have Shamanic ways of calling up energy. The American Indians and ancient Hawaiians used songs to call up energy.

"So how do you learn music?" he declared to the class. "Practice every day for fifteen minutes. When people play music for fame, it sounds shallow and uninspired. But when people play music with an attitude of service, it sounds wonderful! Listen to J.S. Bach; he said that the sole purpose of music is none other than the glorification of God." We all sat enraptured by his words as he continued.

"The tempo of the earth is 60 beats a minute. This beat has a healing quality to it. The tempo aligns your body with the earth; it makes you feel at home—the planet has a heartbeat. People have noticed the heartbeat is getting faster. They say it's due to global warming." Rama's ideas captivated me as his lecture took different forms.

After class, we sat and chatted together for a while.

"Good to see you here, Katie. How do you feel...well rested?" asked Rama, laying down his instrument.

"Yeah, and I'm looking forward to connecting with nature today," I offered.

"That's great. I love nature. Reminds me of that time I started the 1989 California Earthquake. An African Shaman once shared a powerful dance with me, and one night I reveled in that dance, shouting, 'Shaaaango! Shaaaango!' I should not have been messing with those energies. Then the earthquake happened, and the Bay Bridge collapsed. That was my bad."

Rama then promptly rose and disappeared into the house, looking solemn. *Courage*, I thought.

Later that day Aria, Crystal, Alex, Michael, and Josh decided to hike down to the beach through the jungle trail. I had not been to the beach yet and wanted to see it for myself so that I knew the way and could find my way back alone if I needed to.

Forest, the man I had met the previous evening, decided to join us on the hike. He was six feet tall and slender, with a refined, polished look about him. Clean cut and English, with chestnut wavy hair, he must have been about my age. The hike was peculiar. I felt sexual energy the entire time flashing between Forest, me, and the two male Woofers. Aria and Michael had their own special chemistry sparking.

The men made me feel sexy, alive, and brimming with powerful feminine energy. I could not help but feel good that each of them desired me. I was hooked on the attention, like an addict that could not get enough of it. I became an attention-whore. As we crunched and cracked our way through the jungle path in the morning heat, I wondered if it was due to the tantra love vibrations that penetrated the Huelo grounds. It seemed to me to be the best medicine.

If Richard could see me now! Forest entertained me the entire hike. He was very charming. "I'm taking a break from my start-up company. Been having too many problems with stress, and I was on the verge of a nervous breakdown. I had to get away for a while," he told me, holding back a swath of plants in my path.

As I stepped down from a ridge, I tripped over a tree root in the uneven path. In one suave movement, Forest grabbed me and pulled me close. His eyes bore into mine, and I could feel his breath on my cheek.

I tried to explain on the beach that morning that I was on a journey of self-discovery. I think it might have made him even more excited about dating me. So it was with a twinge of guilt that I met him for dinner wearing a light blue summer dress. We ended up in downtown Haiku at Lilikoi Grill, a local spot; he drove us there.

We were seated at a table decked out in a white tablecloth and finished with a bunch of tropical flowers. "Google is going to buy our company in the next five months," Forest told me between bites of sashimi, "but our new CEO has been making things difficult. That's why I came here to reconnect with tantra and renew my spirit."

"Why didn't I experience any new age stuff when I lived in Northern California?" I asked, enjoying my Kalua pork. "I could have used it."

"You weren't hanging around the right people. You need open-minded influences in your life to grow."

"True. There was no spiritual life outside of church when I was a child," I mused, sipping on my wine.

He ate with a kind of desperate ferocity. I could see he was a very high-strung man. I wondered then if he was the kind to transform into a control freak given the chance. When the bill came, I had to pay for half of it, which I was not expecting. For so much wealth and success, he was very careful to avoid paying for our date.

Even though I had already decided not to sleep with any men while on Maui, I placed Forest firmly in the friend-zone after that evening. Call me old fashioned, but a lady asked on a date should not have to pay for it.

We traded Maui hitchhiking stories as it was a kind of tradition to get and give lifts from strangers here. Thanks to my many holidays on the island, I had my fair share of stories. "You can't really pick people up anymore though, too many weirdoes and people on drugs," Forest said, checking his watch as he drove us home. As we were driving, we came upon a dark-looking Italian man, someone who could very well have fallen into the "weirdo" category.

"I don't believe it. Is that...is that Shiva?"

"Who?" I asked Forest as the car slowed.

"Oh my god, it is." He brought the car to a stop and rolled down his window. A man with a long scarf wrapped around his head paused and then beamed at us.

"Looking for a lift, Shiva?" Forest asked.

"I am. Do I know you? Where are you heading?" said the slender, dark, handsome, shirtless man in cotton pants. He opened the car door and piled inside.

"You are Shiva, the yoga teacher, are you not?" asked Forest, taking off again in the car.

"I am. But I like to think of myself as a teacher for all things, not just yoga," said Shiva, laying his bag on the car seat and settling in. In truth, I was nervous to have a strange pirate-looking man behind me. After all, I barely knew Forest that well.

"You won't remember me, but maybe you will remember my girlfriend," said Forest, a curious smile on his face.

"I teach a lot of people, my friend," Shiva responded.

"We booked a private yoga class with you. She showed up naked. You were very gracious about the whole thing."

"Ah yes, I remember her downward dog. What a lovely, young woman." I couldn't help but giggle as Forest went on to explain that she was too spirited for him and that they had to break up some months after that. "It wasn't that I disliked her confidence but rather my preference for being the only person who had seen her naked."

Shiva returned with us to the Bamboo Malu House and settled in right away. He never touched substances or alcohol but instead was high on life and super energized. He was a nomadic wanderer—going wherever the wind took him. We discovered he had a real passion for raw food, yoga, seeking out joy, freedom, ecstatic dancing, and sensual experiences. "Life is juicy. I have made love to at least 25 women this year."

I responded, "Wow, that is a lot of lovers, and the year is not yet over. Four months to go...."

"It does not make it sexual, Katie. I am making a soul connection with each of these goddesses. There is a difference."

That night he, Rama, and the other Shiva disappeared into conversation. Turns out Shiva is a very popular name on this side of the island, but even Rama was tickled by the presence of two Italian yoga-teaching Shivas. "It's a sign that we should be focusing more on the healing nature of our morning yoga," he declared to the house. I excused myself from their company, and Forest bowed, his eyes meeting mine as he kissed me on the hand to bid me good evening.

As I closed my bedroom door and collapsed onto the bed, I found myself filled with a new positive energy. It did not matter that Forest was money conscious or that he was too highly strung for me. It did not matter, because I had no plans to fall in love with him. He was just a friend, someone to flirt with and talk to in this magical place.

Rama had managed to fix the Internet connection, so I was finally able to connect and send emails. As I waited for them to be delivered into my inbox, a thought occurred to me. If I was just having fun and getting to know people, it would not hurt me to email Thomas, the man from the airport. After all, no man had made me feel so strongly attracted to him in some time.

Aloha Thomas,

It was great meeting you at the airport bar the other day. I have landed on Maui and am boarding at a commune house called the Lotus Retreat and Farm. The people here are amazing and free spirited. This will be a good place for me to collect stories for my novel.

So far, I have had a heart reading and explored some of the jungle and beach. I've taken a music class with Rama, the owner of the farm. He is a cool character! It's a small world. This evening we picked up a man who teaches yoga, on the way back from a restaurant, and it turns out he knows some of our guests.

I plan on taking a lot more classes and doing a lot more exploring while I am here.

How's the shoe business?

Katie, the Cosmo Queen

I clicked "Send" and tucked myself in for another night alone in the Bamboo Malu House.

Chapter 4

A Forest of Tantra

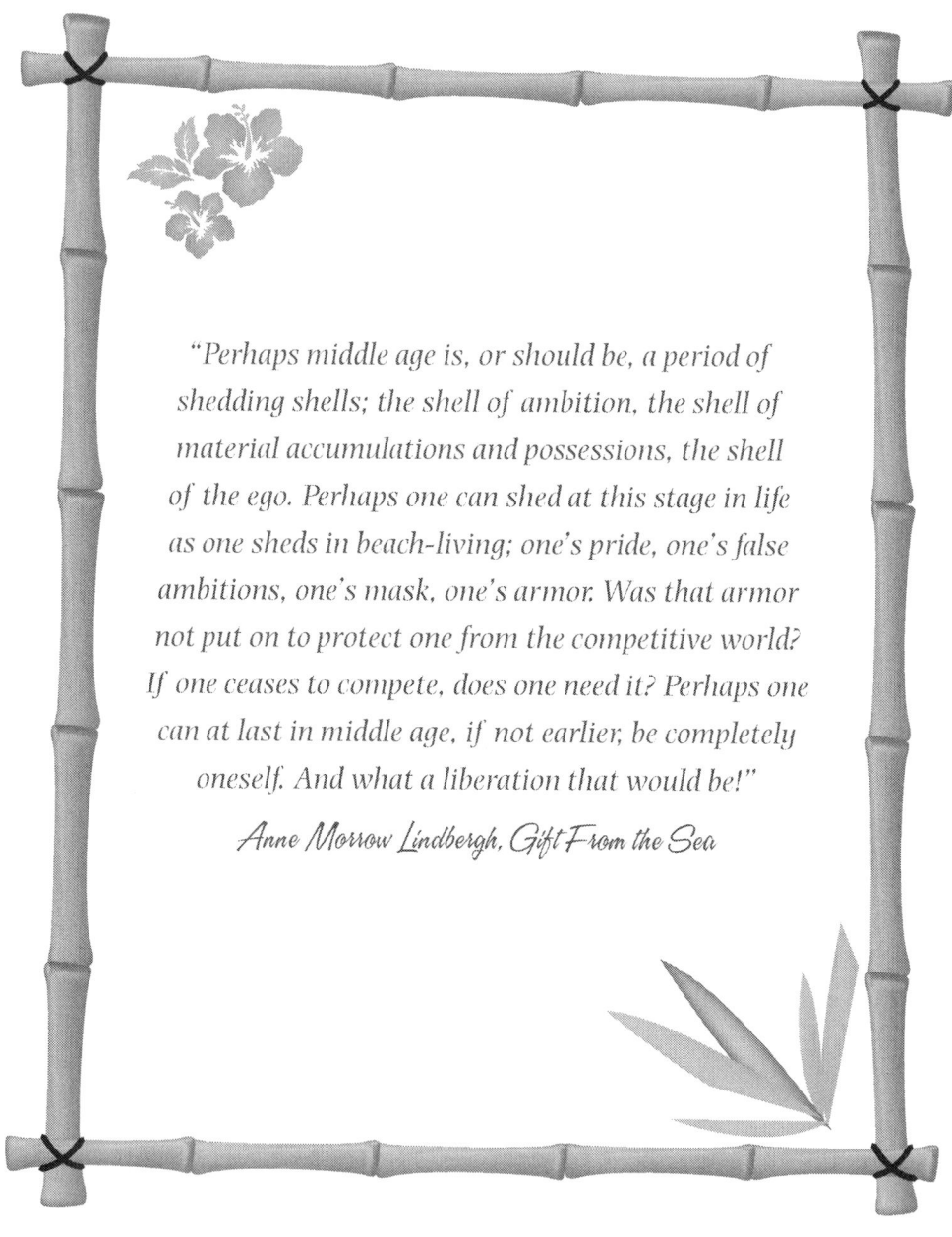

"Perhaps middle age is, or should be, a period of
shedding shells; the shell of ambition, the shell of
material accumulations and possessions, the shell
of the ego. Perhaps one can shed at this stage in life
as one sheds in beach-living; one's pride, one's false
ambitions, one's mask, one's armor. Was that armor
not put on to protect one from the competitive world?
If one ceases to compete, does one need it? Perhaps one
can at last in middle age, if not earlier, be completely
oneself. And what a liberation that would be!"

Anne Morrow Lindbergh, Gift From the Sea

The next few days at the Lotus Retreat and Farm were an adjustment. I slotted into the thick of commune life, building a schedule around the movements of the other people in the house. Each morning there were delicious smells as the Woofers cooked beneath me and gentle music would emanate from one of Rama's early morning music classes.

On this particular morning, I woke to peculiar screaming—a gravelly, raw human roar that made my insides clench. Tumbling out of bed and hitting the floor with an unceremonious thud, I gathered my toiletries and made a dash for the door, thinking that something awful was happening.

The Sounds of Freedom

As the door swung open, Aria glided past with that ever-serene smile on her face, a toothbrush poking from her lips. "Morning, Katie," she said. Stopping in her tracks, she added, "Are you all right? You look stressed."

She was right. I stood in the doorway shielding myself from the imaginary attacker as the yells cycled through the house. "Who's screaming?" I asked, mildly gasping for air from the adrenaline of being woken by visceral cries.

"Oh, don't mind that," she said, taking off again. "Rama is leading Forest in a private music session downstairs. He's just screaming out the pain." A flick of a towel and Aria disappeared down the passage. I gathered myself, repeating Aria's words in my mind. Screaming out the pain? It sounded...therapeutic.

Still rattled by the sound reverberating from Forest downstairs, I approached the card table and took one. "Clarity," it said. I hastily showered and dressed, interested to catch some of the performance downstairs, but by the time I had arrived, it was over. Forest was sitting at the breakfast table, gulping down forkfuls of egg and multicolored leaves.

He smiled at me jovially through his masticating cheeks and continued eating. Rama was there too, and I got my usual morning sing-song greeting from the Woofers. Alex was standing at the stove shirtless, a statue of healthy and rippling muscles. I do believe I had come to enjoy seeing him cook that way.

"Give him extra, Alex," Rama said, pointing a salad fork at Forest. "He screamed through a lot of calories earlier." I settled between Forest and Rama and was immediately given a hot plate of eggs, bacon, tomato, and mushrooms. While heaping salad onto my plate, we chatted lightly, and I wondered what my day would bring.

"I am so ready for the tantra," said Forest, satisfied by his extra-large breakfast, "but, if you don't mind, Crystal, it would be wonderful to try it with Katie." Crystal had flopped down at the table too.

"Tantra? With me?" I said, swallowing the last of my bacon. "Is it sexual?"

"No, no, no," Rama interjected, looking gleeful. "Well yes, but no," he added, rising from the table. "You'll love it, Katie."

Forest was staring at me expectantly, but Rama had given me nothing to go on. *You're not dating him*, I reminded myself, and some of the nerves subsided. I reminded myself to go with the flow and keep an open mind.

"Sure, let's do it, as long as it doesn't get raunchy."

"No promises," said Forest, a devilish look in his eye. I rose with him, and together with Rama, we adjourned to the music room.

The room was covered in seating mats and plump floor pillows. I was nervous, and the food in my stomach knew it. Sunlight streamed in through the windows, casting gentle leaf-shaped patterns on the walls and floor. I had always wanted to try tantra, and I guess this was the time. Crystal told me tantric practices do not necessarily involve sex.

I held my breath and hoped I had agreed to a non-sexual encounter with Forest. It could have gone either way. But my mind was open, and my heart was ready, so I settled across from him, crossing my legs. He mirrored my position and pushed his knees up against mine. Contact. I exhaled the nerves.

Forest looked elated from his early morning scream session. Much of his nervous demeanor had vanished, which was unfortunate because it made him more attractive. Rama settled some distance from us, a voice in the wilderness. "Tantra is not technique! Tantra is a path of the heart. A master is one who knows that whatever is happening, whatever has happened or is going to happen, is perfect for your spiritual growth. Tantra is a way of being," he stated then some minutes later added, "It uses chakras, mantra, asana, pranayama, and ritual ceremony to address many things. Now breathe deeply together, and hold eye contact."

I met Forest's eyes and realized they were a pale blue. I sat up straight, and together we breathed deeply, inhaling and exhaling several times. I looked away. "Gaze softly into my eyes, Katie. I will do the same. This is a connection exercise, so we can't break contact. Focus on your breathing, and clear your mind of thoughts," he said to me.

I realized he had done this before. I wondered how many of the women in the house had sat across from him in this position. It did not matter, I reminded myself again. Staring into the pale eyes of a software engineer was awkward for me. It felt deeply intimate. Thoughts rose inside my mind and tried to make their way out of my mouth.

"How..." I started.

"Sshhhh," Rama said, his own eyes closed in concentration. I was overwhelmed with anxiety and fear, and in the next second, it was replaced with an urge to laugh. After five minutes, that too, passed, and I found my mind finally quieting down. Time stretched into his eyes and encircled us.

Just as I had acquired some peace, Forest spoke. "May I touch your knees?" The yes came out of me before the thought did. Was this a trick? It felt so natural. My thoughts were slower now, although in the back of my mind, I still wondered if something inappropriate would happen. *Please do not let this get out of hand*, I thought, sending the wish into the universe.

More time passed, and Forest asked to hold my hands. All the while, his pale eyes were like icecaps boring into mine. A strange sense of peace washed over me. Soon after that a warmth or energy welled up in my lower extremities. I tried to deny it, but it was useless—it felt sexual. "Can I place my hand on your heart? Will you place your hand on mine?"

I nodded and moved into position. His hand was warm, even through my cotton top. It was an intense feeling, a world beneath the touch. Tears filled Forest's eyes, and I found that mine followed naturally. There was a deep sadness in him; it was...beautiful. In that moment, I knew him and trusted him. He was a kind soul.

"That's it!" said Rama from the blind oblivion outside of Forest and me. It jarred me out of the connection, and we repossessed our hands. It was over. A strange buzzing sensation stayed with me for a few minutes. The session was only 30 minutes long, but it felt much longer than that. Forest left in a hurry, his eyes still glassy from the experience.

I thanked him, and we hugged. "It's my last day. I'm leaving for the Grand Wailea Hotel tomorrow morning. That was the first time I've ever connected with a woman like that," he told me, ducking behind the door and vanishing. I did not know what Forest had found in the room with me, but I was glad it made him happy. Everyone deserves happiness.

Feeling relaxed and wide open, I decided it was a good time to head down to one of the old Tiki temples Rama had been telling me about the day before. Sita had brought back sacred wood from Indonesia so that she could rebuild the temples on Maui, on the Lotus Farm. I made my way down the winding jungle path with my bag and writing gear, the sound of insects humming as I walked.

Time at the Temple

Sita and Rama had done an exceptional job of rebuilding the temples. Now they stood as monuments to creativity and artistic expression—the perfect place for me to practice meditation and write. Rama told me that the wood carried hundreds of years' worth of prayers and that it was imbibed into the cellular fiber of the place.

I headed to the smaller of the two temples, hoping to find it empty. It was a fair walk, but the temple overlooked a cliff that invited in the most amazing ocean view. I stepped inside the wooden structure with its benches and squashy pillows in ornate designs. This was a peaceful place, although it was not as fancy as the larger temple close to the house.

Large decorative tapestries hung off the walls, recalling spiritualism from other countries. Gloriously, I had it all to myself. The first thing I did was walk around the place, admiring the god and goddess statues, and, of course, to check for any Wi-Fi signals. As if it came from the creative gods themselves, I found a spot where the signal was strong. I set up my laptop and put my phone in front of me. I wrote what I learned from Rama about tantra:

Yoga, Taoist, and Healing masters had simple techniques for strengthening the immune system and creating longevity, I scribbled furiously. When these techniques are empowered by the heart, they become miraculous. In Tantra, there is a lot of weaving and merging going on—not only with the earth and each other but with the divine as well. That is what love is, the recognition that you and I are the same.

Unity creates power. The more unified a person, the more powerful they are. The more unified a family or a country, the more power exists there. Power creates freedom and the ability to choose for yourself. Tantra is about opening yourself to love. When you walk, you consciously massage the earth with your feet, and God is there. When you are totally with someone, God is there. When you are in a lovers' embrace, God is there. We are all hunting for the Holy Spirit. I wrote, ending by underlining the word spirit.

Brightly colored flags were dotted around the room, and the books lined the walls in places. Now some meditation. Since arriving at the Bamboo Malu House, I had noticed how much value everyone placed in the act of meditating. I had always believed in the power of meditation but could never quite get it right.

My mind was always racing away from me with ideas and insights. I folded my legs and closed my eyes. Peaceful. Now relax. I should probably write about this place though, so I peeked at my laptop screen. Okay, plenty of time. Don't worry. Relax. *I wonder what Thomas is doing right now? He would love it here. No! Don't think*, I told myself.

After 20 minutes of broken meditation, I decided to stand and do some yoga stretches. A voice sounded behind me, and I shrieked in fright. It was Rama. He was wearing a loin cloth, a tiny piece of material that barely covered him, and his face was painted blue. "That was the worst attempt at meditating I've ever seen," he said to me, smiling.

"How long have you been sitting there?" I asked him, clutching my heart.

"You should try meditating before you open your laptop. Even better, don't open it." He lifted himself off the wooden beam and sauntered inside as I watched his blue-smeared face. He had tied his long hair into a top knot, and it waggled about freely as he walked. I tried very hard not to look at his loin cloth.

"Write with pen on paper," Rama declared, feeling one of his purple flags that hung across a statue. "Or you could meditate first then write in another spot."

I rounded on him. "What are you doing here?"

"I was getting ready for my weekly jungle walk when I saw you come in here. Thought I would stop by and thank you for what you did for Forest this morning. I think he released a lot more frustration with you than he did with me screaming." Rama pursed his lips and held his chin as he leaned back on the statue.

"No thanks necessary. I was glad to help."

"You know, meditation is only the first step into the unknown. There is a universe inside yourself, if you care to find it." I settled on the wooden bench across from him, in wonder of this confident, wild man. "The last time I was in California recording music, my beloved Sita was in Bali on one of her many spiritual travels. I believed I was all right. Mr. 'overly independent' she calls me. But the time passed, and I began to miss her. She and I are entwined souls dancing in eternity. My body ached for her touch. My ears strained for her voice. My eyes expected her face at every turn. My music suffered without her. Eventually, I told myself, enough! I could just leave my body and go to see her. I lay on the ground in the center of my apartment and started my circular breathing..."

"Astral projection?" I asked, and he nodded.

"I melted into nothing. I found myself 100 miles above the earth! I flew to Sita over the Pacific Ocean and saw the sun rise over the earth."

I watched as he told me his story, his dirt-smeared body a pantomime of memory. He was so passionate about his journey. "And do you know what happened? I came across a blue whale. 'I have to go!' I said to the whale, 'My wife is waiting for me.' But the whale had a lesson to impart. He showed me music and the unlimited scales of the ocean vibrations. He taught me that music is like the number pi, infinite and never-ending. Several months later my wife and I met a scientist who had written a book about the scientific study of whale sounds. And on the cover of the book...just one symbol: pi. So there you go."

"Did you find your way to Sita in the end?" I asked.

"Oh no. But I found what I was looking for. The next morning, I made some of my greatest music."

"That's incredible," I said, not wanting to sound like a skeptic. "Can I learn to astral project?"

"Depends."

"On what?"

He walked across the temple and took a book off the shelf. "Your ability to release control. I wanted to see Sita, but I needed to finish my music. The Universe gave me what I needed, not what I wanted."

"You think I can't release control?" I asked him, confused and a little offended.

"I am sure that you think you can, but for something like astral projection, pretending is not enough."

He paged through an old book that was covered in dust from years of sitting in the beachside temple. "You really believe it's possible?" I asked him, betraying my skepticism.

"Oh, I believe in a lot more than that. The last time Sita's parents came to visit, I was listening to music on my headphones and could hear her father coughing from the next room. I knew he must be in a lot of discomfort. Without thinking, I told the angels to help Papi and ease his pain. Immediately, I heard a great whooshing sound, and the coughing stopped. When I poked my head in to check what had happened, I saw them—angels in a circle above his head, sending him peace."

I could see that Rama was enraptured by this experience and believed it wholeheartedly. "Amazing," I said with a note of sadness, thinking of my own life. Here was a man who had explored the limits of his creativity, and he had spoken to whales and commanded angels.

"And you can't even meditate," Rama said, almost finishing my thought for me.

"I will work on it," I said as he moved to the door.

"See that you do. Close your eyes, and simply breathe deeply and slowly. Thoughts will come and go—release them. Be present...it's really that simple.... This place could give you everything you ever needed if you let it. Get out of your own way."

With that, his waggling bun whipped from the temple, and I heard him break out in heavy whooping noises as he disappeared into the jungle.

Inspired by his pep talk, I decided to do something more physical to get my body moving. I packed up my laptop and phone and headed towards the long, jagged dirt path to the beach below. Breathing in the clean ocean air was exhilarating. *Clarity*, I thought. I spent a long time walking up and down the beach. I took Rama's advice and cleared my mind of thoughts about my ex-fiancé and my predicament.

It was rejuvenating. Exercise itself could be so spiritual. I wrote for a time on the rocks by the shoreline and the cascading green cliffs, staring out over the infinite and thinking about Rama's whale spirit guide. I wondered if I would ever find one. Could I ever let go of control? Could I just be without needing a man to love me? Who was I now, in this place?

Chance Encounters in Paradise

Some of the Woofers poured onto the beach for their daily sunset ritual, although it was at least two hours before the sun would descend from the sky and crossover to the opposite side of the island. With them was a man I had never seen before. I noticed him immediately; he was very handsome and confident. I was working on centering and balance and stood in a tree pose. I noticed him gravitating over to me.

"You're Katie," he said to me, and I nodded. "I'm Chris. Can I join you?"

"Sure," I said, lowering my arms and leg.

"Great form, by the way," he said, his golden body gleaming in the darkening sunlight. *Oh god, he's flirting with me.*

"Thanks."

"Crystal was telling me about your book. You some kind of famous writer?"

I blinked at him a few times more than I would have liked. "Not yet, but I'm working on it. That's why I'm here. Where are you from?"

He hiked up his shorts to squeeze the last vitamin D out of the sun. Clearly, he cared about his youthful tan. "From Tennessee. I'm here to trim trees for the electric company. Down here for six months when I met Crystal. She's great, such a free spirit."

"Yeah, she is," I mused, considering this young man.

He was around 33 years old with strawberry blonde hair and green eyes. "Are you a free spirit?" he asked.

"The best kind," I said back, flirting a little.

I got a strong sense that he wanted me to find him attractive, which was overwhelmingly easy. He leaned over to pick up stones as he spoke, flexing his muscles unnecessarily. "Listen, would you join me for dinner tonight? We can meet at Charley's Restaurant & Saloon in Paia."

Wow, not five minutes of conversation and he wanted to take me out. What had the Woofers told him about me? Flattered, I agreed to meet him there in an hour. "Just gotta drop some of the tree cuttings at the depo; then I will meet you there," he said, blowing me a kiss and winking. Once he had left, I hurried back up the trail and down the path to the Bamboo Malu House.

I did not have much time to get ready; a quick shower, brush of my hair, and some lipstick would do. Women on Maui do not fuss and worry about makeup; it is about being natural. In any event, Chris had seen me sweaty on the beach, and I had no intention of sleeping with him. This was just a nice date with a nice boy. I mean man. As I left I noticed Rama, back in his normal flowing clothes, clean-faced, welcoming two new guests into the house.

The words would come if I just kept playing and living life. That was what I was doing and loving every moment. With that thought, I got into my economy blueberry and sped off into town. I would be lying if I pretended that I was not flattered by Chris's attention. *Do young men really find older woman attractive*, I wondered. But then, this was Maui. Anything could happen. Was I fooling myself? Clarity.

Desperate to calm myself down and limit the excitement of the chance encounter on the beach, I dashed into Charley's and was directed to a table. There sat the now fully clothed Chris in a casual shirt and chinos. Only he was not alone. With him was an even younger man with dark hair and a budding goatee.

A New Kind of Double Date

"Chris?" I said, trying to still my breath.

"Hi!" Chris sprang up and pulled out my chair for me. "Katie! I'm glad you came. I hope you don't mind, but I invited Mike to join us. He is my roommate for the next six months." Chris slid in the chair, and I greeted Mike. He was looking at me with a mixture of confusion and projected desire.

We spoke about the island and the best places to go in the area. Chris kept ordering drink after drink, which made conversation easy. As the evening progressed, I relaxed, becoming more and more animated as I shared my Maui stories.

Though I was older, I felt like a desirable woman around these two young men, who were exceedingly charming. More than once I wondered why, until the end of the evening came. The three of us headed back to our cars after Chris had graciously paid for my dinner (*Forest could learn a thing or two*, I thought in the back in my mind), and the moment came.

"Katie, would you like to come back with us, to our place?" Chris asked me, his eyes shining in the moonlight.

"Your place? With the two of you?" I repeated to myself as I was digging for my car keys. Then, somewhere in my mind, something clicked. "Oh!" I said aloud, realizing what had been happening the entire night.

Here were two men who wanted a sexual experience with an older woman. Chris, in his charming manner, was asking me for a three way. A fit of giggles overtook me as I fell back onto my car. "I'm sorry, boys. I'm sorry. I had a wonderful dinner tonight, but I can't accompany you home this...this...evening," I said, trying desperately not to laugh.

I could see they were disappointed, but they were gracious

about the misunderstanding. I arrived home that evening full of energy. "Still got it!" I said, throwing my keys on the counter and collapsing onto my bed. If I could still stir the sexual interest of two virile young men, perhaps Rama was right; I just needed to let go and focus on what I needed in my life.

Somewhat tired, I opened my laptop, and there was an email waiting for me from none other than Thomas, the airport hunk. Alive after a night of flirting, I read the email and responded in kind, perhaps a little more outrageously than I had planned.

Aloha Katie,

It sounds like you have found a little slice of heaven over there. I'd love to see it. I went on a corporate hike with Mr. Yamahito and our marketing team through the hills of Kyoto.

We stopped at the red Ginkaku Temple, and I thought of you on Maui, in your temple by the ocean. The marketing team got the hike sponsored by one of our women's brands, so I spent the day in the most violently purple shoes I've ever worn. Thought you would get a laugh out of that.

If I close this deal soon, I should finish up here early. You have been on my mind lately, and I have been enjoying your emails. What a blessing to connect with a woman of your obvious charm and character over a brief meeting at the airport.

Have an excellent day. I will email you tomorrow.

XXX Thomas, the Airport King

Aloha Thomas!

Just had an interesting experience with a couple of young men over dinner. I barely escaped with my virginity intact! Needless to say, I will be more careful next time when choosing my dinner guests.

Japan sounds wonderful, and I would have loved to have seen you in those purple shoes. I bet you had all the ladies in your marketing team checking out your shapely legs. ;)

You should consider joining me on Maui if you finish your deal early. You work too hard and need a bit of a break! Plus, I have selfish reasons for wanting you here.

I will email you in the morning when I am more composed.

Have a wonderful evening.

Katie, the Cosmo Queen X

Chapter 5

Finding a New Home

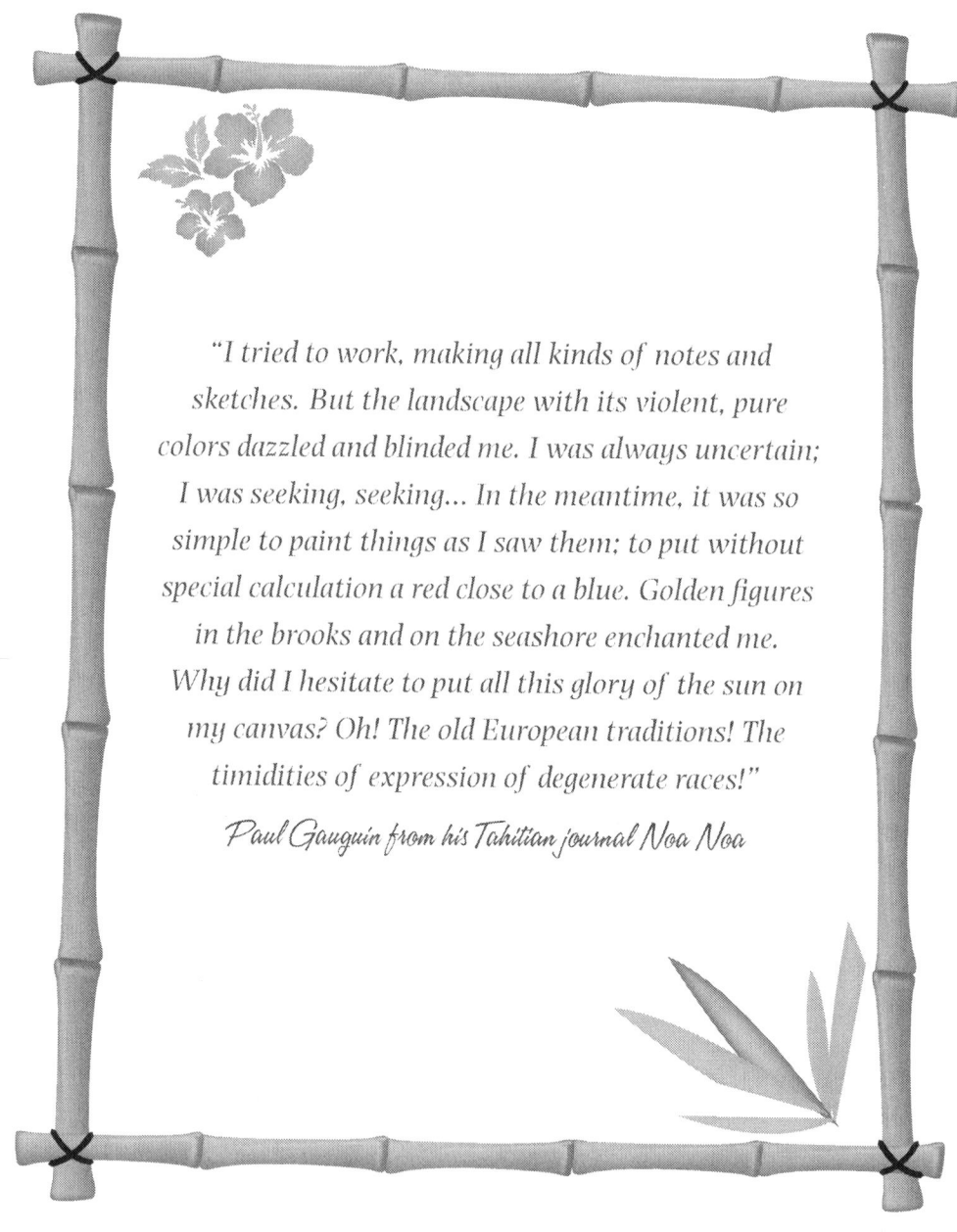

"I tried to work, making all kinds of notes and sketches. But the landscape with its violent, pure colors dazzled and blinded me. I was always uncertain; I was seeking, seeking... In the meantime, it was so simple to paint things as I saw them; to put without special calculation a red close to a blue. Golden figures in the brooks and on the seashore enchanted me. Why did I hesitate to put all this glory of the sun on my canvas? Oh! The old European traditions! The timidities of expression of degenerate races!"

Paul Gauguin from his Tahitian journal Noa Noa

Settling into life in the Bamboo Malu House was easy. The daily routines and classes were always brimming with happy faces and open hearts. It was strange waking up each morning with nothing to do, all the while knowing that I had to find a permanent place to live before my three months in paradise were up.

I enjoyed the Woofers most of all, with their cheerful attitudes and willingness to help. Since arriving, Aria had met a nice young man, a fellow woofer, Michael, and the two of them had invited love into the house. I would often see them stealing kisses along the path as I made my way down to the temples every day. I observed Michael being giddy around her. He picked flowers from the garden, and she placed them in her long golden hair. Their love was innocent and pure. This inspired me and the other visiting female guests. Sita would soon be back from one of her trips abroad, and Rama had busied himself making sure that everything would be perfect for her return.

Faith as a Reckless Driver

A new guest had joined the house, a fiery young woman by the name of Faith Blossom. She was taking singing lessons from Rama and, at age 33, was an independent spirit from the moment I met her.

Faith had long red hair and brown eyes, dark enough to make her look mysterious and strange—even to the Woofers in the house, who treated her carefully, like a fragile package delivered to the house that read, "This way up." It was clear that she was opinionated and spirited.

Her clothes and makeup enhanced her natural mystery; she wore mainly dark dresses and dark lipsticks. She claimed to be a very spiritual woman. Nothing seemed to scare Faith, which is why I found her so delightful. One day after her singing lesson, she invited me for ice cream. That was when I discovered her particular proclivity for reckless driving.

The drive to the ice cream parlor was slower than I would have liked. Faith said, "I got a speeding ticket. It ain't going to happen again." She drove the varying posted speed limits precisely: 15, 25 and 35 miles on the one lane highway leading to town. I was nervous as cars had to slow down to avoid hitting us. Impatient drivers honked and passed on the opposite side of the road.

I clutched my seat, my anxiety rising, but the real action happened on the way back. Impatient to eat her ice cream, she reversed out of her spot in the parking lot, flattening several waste bins that had been neatly arranged on the curb. She said, "I'm really short and couldn't see." She almost pulled off her back bumper, and she was completely sober. We took off through town, stopping at the beach to enjoy the cones.

When I pointed out the damage that the waste bin accident had done to her car, Faith simply shrugged and said, "That was there already." But that was Faith—she did not let unimportant things like waste bins and minor car accidents ruin her nice time. I respected that.

We got into her car to drive home. I was a little nervous with the hiccupping and driving. She told me that she gets hiccups at night and in this higher altitude. "Should I drive? Are you okay?" I asked.

"No, I'm fine, and I prefer to drive my own car. If I ever felt like I could not drive, I would ask you."

It was a painfully slow drive on the Hana Highway due to Faith's extra careful driving. As we slowly rounded a bend in the road, I saw an animal moving that had been struck. Instead of swerving to avoid it, she somehow managed to drive over the half living animal...thump, thump. She did the final sacrifice. "Oh my god, did you see that thing? Oh holy crap Was that a raccoon? I think I just killed a raccoon. I feel so bad...oh my god. I can't believe it. It came outta nowhere.... Shit Did you see it?"

"No," I lied, "but I felt it...it's in a better place now," I added, reading her distress. Nothing could be done, and I was not a fan of road kill. "Anyone could have run over it." I was amazed how she could not see it as we were approaching at such a slow speed. For a spiritual woman, she was cussing up a storm. "By the way, that was probably a cat or something. We don't have raccoons on the island," I corrected her.

Like me, Faith was called to the island. She watched the very same Luscious Life Tour program on the Internet and found her way to Rama and Sita. To earn money, she walked the restaurants in town and sold flower leis to tourists. This allowed her extra income to pursue her dream of becoming a recording artist. Faith and I fell in step soon after meeting each other.

I liked her and she liked me, and suddenly we were close. That happens sometimes with kindred spirits. Either way, I knew she had a part to play in my future here on Maui.

The Healing Powers of Scream Therapy

The morning was unforgivably sunny as it was so often, and Crystal and Aria knocked on my bedroom door as I was sitting by the window taking a moment to complete my journaling for the day. I opened the door. "Time for a good stress release. We thought you would like to come," said wild-eyed Crystal.

"Where are you guys off to this early?" I asked, putting down my pen.

"Alex just broke up with his boyfriend, so we are heading down to the screaming cliffs—Josh is coming too. We thought you'd like to join," said Aria, a pretty arrangement of flowers in her hair. "Faith is coming too." At that, I rose, and together we walked the twenty-minute trail to the cliffs, where my temple stood only a few yards away.

The sky was a clear, blinding blue, and I could hear the waves lapping at the beach below. I had not realized that Alex was gay, although now that I had discovered this, it made perfect sense. He was very flirty and wholly disinterested, which only made me more attracted to him in the beginning. But he had never crossed the line into overt sexual commentary.

Faith was in a sullen mood, but the prospect of a good scream seemed to invigorate her. Together, we lined up at the railing and formed a chain of knitted hands. "What now?" Faith asked after a few awkward moments of breathing. The Woofers had closed their eyes and were smiling at the sun. Alex cracked an eye at her question then shouted, "I thought you were a nice guy, but you lied! Lying liar! The cliffs can have you!"

His voice was full of power and emotion. I watched as his eyes glazed over. Immediately after he was done, the next voice rang out into the distance. "I am tired of not having any money! I need to get off the weed!" shouted Crystal, smiling.

"I have a headache!" screamed Josh as it echoed around us. "I want it to stop!"

It was Aria's turn next. "I want to travel, but I've fallen in love with the farm!" she shouted. Faith waited patiently for her turn. A moment hung in the air between Aria's shout and hers before she screamed, "I wish the world was a better place! I wish I was a better person!" Then, almost in slow motion, all eyes turned to me.

I had been so enthralled by the shouting I had forgotten to come up with something to scream about. Then it struck me: "I want to learn to love myself, but I think I'm falling for Thomas instead! I need to stick to my vows!" The frustration boomed out of me, and I knew it was the truth. I had shouted it clearly and with courage, and I felt lighter for it.

After my scream had echoed into the sea, we all clapped for each other and settled down on some nearby rocks. Alex brought some beer, Josh had some weed, and Faith produced a hip flask of whiskey that had been so well concealed I didn't know where on her it had come from. "So those are the screaming cliffs, eh?" she said, swigging the whiskey then offering it to me.

"Good times."

The screaming cliffs were a memory I would never forget. Life was good now, and I was happy. I had friends, enriching experiences, love, admiration, and attention from the opposite sex. I felt like I had everything. Everything...but a man. Thomas had been on my mind since I escalated the flirting that night with my alcohol-fueled email, but he was ever the gentleman.

I found myself more and more entranced by his charm and sensibility, and I desperately wanted to see him again in person despite myself.

Shopping for a New Residence

The next day I needed to find a new home as my time was running out at the Lotus Retreat. I called Henry, a man I had met at a Zeptember concert—he was looking for a roommate for his Paia home.

My new friend at the Lotus Retreat, Linda, a visiting New York cop, came with me. Linda said, "He could be a predator." I highly doubted it but entertained it all the same. The truth was, anything could happen, and I was glad for Linda's company.

We found the house and strolled up the garden path to the front door. Linda rapped on it hard, eager to defuse the danger. Henry opened the door, but he looked nothing like he had at the concert. With clear blue eyes and dark grey hair in two lopsided ponytails, a tight tank top, and leopard print shorts, he looked like something out of an '80s aerobics video.

As we crossed the threshold of his home, a thick pillar of smoke engulfed us. Henry seated us on a torn brown couch and offered us something to drink and homemade pot brownies, which we politely declined. He bustled off to get us water. "Don't forget to smoke a little more while you're in there. I can almost taste oxygen in here," she called after him in a low voice that only I could hear. "Can you believe the nerve of that guy? I feel stoned already."

"I'm starting to get the impression that this is not the best place for me," I whispered. "We'll hear him out then leave before we start seeing red lizards on the walls."

Henry came back into the room with an ancient dog following. she looked older than the tattered couch we were sitting on. She was baring her teeth like she was growling, but no noise did she emit.

"Is your dog friendly? Why is she growling?" I asked nervously.

"No, she is always smiling," Henry responded warmly. Then Happy, the dog, flopped down on my legs, clearly exhausted by the movement, and did not move again.

Henry was a sweet, childlike man from the South. We chatted briefly, and it became obvious that he was way too out there for my taste. "I don't drink alcohol...I only smoke pot daily. I hope you don't mind. Did you know that when I first met you at the concert I had taken two hits of acid?"

"No, really? I could not tell," I replied, trying to keep a straight face.

Henry loved to talk and shared more stories. In my head, I

wished he would stop talking before he got himself in trouble. "When I was in the 8th grade, I took a bag of shrooms with me to school and got the entire 8th grade class high." He smiled, fondly remembering those crazy days.

"Maybe we should change the subject," I told him. "My friend here is a New York cop."

Linda was cool. "Hey, not to worry. I used to party when I was younger. Besides, I am here on vacation." We were polite and thanked Henry for his time. I told him I would let him know if I would rent a room by tomorrow.

"I will not let you live with Pippy Longstocking," she said as we kept waving to him as we got into the car, and, hilariously, he kept smiling and waving back.

I said, "He looked so normal when I first met him. His hair was nicely groomed and hung nice and straight on his shoulders. He was dressed preppy in khaki shorts and a button shirt. This is certainly a new look for him."

Linda said, "I'm not surprised. You did say you met him at a Zeptember concert, right?"

The Power Within

It was back to the drawing board. Henry would not be a suitable roommate, and I could never live in a house where 90% of the space was consumed by pot smoke. The drive back to the farm was quick, and we arrived just in time for Shiva One's famous healing class. Since the younger traveling Italian Shiva had arrived, our resident Shiva was affectionately referred to as my number One.

"Ah, Katie, I am glad you are back. Time for some healing, yes?" he said to me as I walked in the door with Linda. I was tired and wanted to go upstairs. Faith saw us come in and had other ideas.

"Oh, yes, she rushed especially to get here in time," she told Shiva One, shoving me forward. "I need to skip class myself tonight. Just going to mosey along down to my room for some shut eye. See you later."

"Me too...need to get up early tomorrow to do more sightseeing," Linda said to me with a wink. "Enjoy your session with Shiva."

Shiva One grabbed me by my wrist, and before I knew it, I was alone with him in a smaller room off the main music room, where we practiced yoga with both Shivas in the mornings. Shiva One had considerably more hair than Shiva Two, and on this occasion, he wore it tied high beneath a red scarf that was wrapped around his head.

A light beard traced around his face. Since Two had arrived, he had decided to grow it a little so that people would be less confused by the name similarity. We settled on some pillows on the floor, and the class began. "We will do a private healing session since you are my only student today. First the lotus position. That's right, you face me. We'll do a bit of breathing now."

I did as instructed, and we began breathing deeply together. "Now lie down on your back and relax," Shiva said. He moved around me, gently rubbing my head and forcing my back to arch. "This will open your heart for me."

"What does it do?" I asked, nervously.

"Let's just say it stirs the psychic resonances. I need those sparks of intuition to help guide you."

I felt fairly self-conscious and was aware of the strong scent of weed drifting off me from Henry's house. It did not seem to bother Shiva One. He began to chant and called the god Ganesh, who favors artists and creative people and is a remover of obstacles. He whispered prayers beneath his breath. He lightly touched my heart then rested his hands on other parts of my body. My heart beat harder in places.

"You are a wonderfully powerful woman," he said softly. "To get your book done, you need to speak from your true feelings;

the truth of your heart will make it successful. But you are also terrible at quieting your mind. Yes, very terrible," he said, smiling sweetly. "You must work hard to remedy the lack of focus you have when meditating."

I wondered briefly if he had been talking to Rama then relaxed into his gentle chanting. "You must practice every morning and every evening. It will help you with your sleep concerns. You have a long spiritual journey and must relearn how to be a child again. And yes...I see it now..."

"What is it?" I asked, afraid of his answer.

"Your heart. You must take responsibility for it. It belongs to you, not someone else. You don't have to give it away. You need to stop looking for a man to validate your life. You are already perfect and worthy of love." It was a profound feeling rippling through me. The healing session was an exceptional experience. I developed a newfound respect for bearded Shiva that day and his mystical power.

The session ended with a key piece of advice: "Use discernment with men. They must earn your respect. Give it another six months or more, Katie...then you might be ready to invite a man into your life again."

I thanked Shiva One for the great session. I did not have cash on me so offered to write a check. "S-h-i-v-a...do you have a last name," I teased, "or just a first name like Prince or Madonna?"

He beamed softly and said in a soft tone, "No. Please write the check to my real name, Anthony Deltano." I later realized that his name Shiva was a name given to him by his spiritual teacher, just like Sita and Rama.

I left the session feeling calm and refreshed and somewhat nervous about my future. Despite what Shiva One had said, I had a date that night. Just another man I had met while shopping.

A Case of Mistaken Caller Identity

Maui was like that...people were not afraid to approach you and ask for a date, no matter where you were on the island. Earlier that week I was at my favorite grocery store in Paia, Mana Foods. Much of their locally grown produce is organic. The store is a treat for the body and soul. They sell products infused with love and spirituality.

You feel the mana and aloha instantly. The aisles are narrow, and you brush against others and smile. I was transported back in time to the flower power generation of the late sixties shopping with peaceful, loving people. I smell the earthy fragrance of Patchouli oil. I see long flowing locks and stylish dreadlocks that adorn slender, tanned bodies. This was where I first met Jason. I found him very attractive; although his hair was thinning already, he had broad shoulders and a muscly frame, which I liked.

No one could wear a Hawaiian shirt quite like Jason could, not Forest, not Alex, and not even the two younger men, Chris and Mike. I had pulled my car into the parking lot of Mana Foods, looking for a space close to the entrance, when Jason came to my rescue. Another driver had claimed the parking spot that I had taken, although it was very obviously mine because I had arrived there first. "Where did you learn how to drive, you stupid bitch!" he yelled at me.

Jason was unpacking his own groceries into his car, right next to my spot. "Don't talk to the lady like that, you ass," he said, bashing on the man's window. I found his defense of my parking spot charming, and well, the rest was history. I was upstairs getting ready for the date we had set when he called. "I'm going to be a little late, Katie. I'm being held up at Costco."

Great, I thought, disappointed. There had been some red flags with Jason in the brief conversation I had enjoyed with him at Mana Foods, but I had already accepted the dinner date. This was just another red flag. I took a deep breath and reminded myself that he was not someone I was going to get romantically involved with, so it did not matter.

We were going as friends and, for me, another new experience, and that was it. Jason had invited me to a friend's BBQ, and I was pleased to be invited. It meant that lots of other people would be there, which I liked. I left my room and descended the stairs to find Rama and Faith in a fake heart reading. "Just as I thought," he said, "no heart."

"You look amazing," Faith said, turning towards me. "All that for a friend? I think you like the attention too much, Katie."

She was not wrong. "No harm in getting dressed up for a friendly Barbeque. I might as well look good."

Rama popped an olive into his mouth, catching Faith's eyes. "It doesn't hurt if Jason turns out to be the one, you mean," said Faith boldly.

I knew she was just teasing me, but again, I felt flustered and transparent so I quickly made my way out of the kitchen and took a seat outside on the wooden beam. Ten minutes passed, then twenty, then forty-five. Jason was very, very late, and every now and then a Woofer would wander by and ask me what I was doing. My nerves were taking over.

I decided to call Jason and let him have it. Flustered and perched in a nice dress on a hard beam, I dialed a number and waited for him to answer.

"Hello?" came the voice on the other side of the call.

"Aloha, Jason, listen, I know you said that you would be late, but I've been sitting outside waiting for you almost an hour now. I mean, what kind of man leaves a lady waiting like this? Maybe we should just cancel at this point because the anticipation of the date is ruined..."

I waited for him to respond, but all I heard was light breathing.

"Say something for yourself," I urged, impatient from all the waiting he had already made me do.

"Ah, hi, Katie. I'm not Jason. I'm Thomas."

The words hit me like a bucket of ice hits a coach at a successful sporting event. "Oh shit. Oh SHIT. I am so, so, so sorry. Thomas?" I looked at the screen of my phone.

"Yeah, it's me."

I could hear that I had offended him. Even though my date was a friendly one, I suddenly felt like a giant whore. "I'm really sorry. Your number is right next to Jason's, a friend that was supposed to take me to a Barbeque tonight."

"It's okay, Katie, really. An easy mistake to make. I'm in the middle of a meeting right now, but I will talk to you later, all right?" his voice sounded stiff and unnatural.

"Okay, sorry again—this is not a real date, and I'm sorry, Jason...I mean Thomas! THOMAS! Shit." And I hung up. I could not believe that had happened.

Things were going so well between Thomas and me, but we had only communicated so far by email. Now here was our first call, and I blew it by accusing him of being another man, another man that I was meeting for a date! He must have thought I was such a slut. I sat there for some time, my hands on my face, my head bowed, thinking. Bearded Shiva's voice wafted through my consciousness. I knew what this guilty feeling was. I was afraid I had ruined my romantic chances with Thomas. Even though I had been denying it all along, with the emails back and forth, I had developed feelings for him. I had imagined what it might be like to be Mrs. Thomas many times. Curses!

This was exactly what Shiva had been talking about. I was not ready for another emotional blow. Getting romantically involved at this point would lead me to nothing but more heartache. I calmed myself down and decided to relax. Jason was *not* my future boyfriend or husband, and neither was Thomas. It did not matter, honest mistake.

With Jason at the BBQ

Night fell as I waited in earnest for that inconsiderate Jason. I thought about the guilt that I felt about going out with another man while Thomas was stuck in a business meeting. I felt like a foolish school girl. My mind said one thing while my heart did another.

As I was waiting and staring at the striking night sky, a light streaked across my view—a shooting star! I watched it dissipate over the tree canopies ahead and reminded myself that I had revirginized and was only here in this place to have fun.

Right after that, a white sedan pulled into the Lotus Farm's parking lot with Jason perched in the front seat. I piled into the car, and off we went. Without so much as an apology for the unimaginable lateness, we stopped at Mana Foods to grab some food for the BBQ.

We chose what we wanted together, and it was a polite exchange. Jason was wearing a navy blue Hawaiian shirt with chinos, which was very appealing. It was hard for me to stay angry with him when I could tell he did not feel that anything was wrong. At the cashier's counter, everything changed however.

Jason bustled me out of the way, which at first I took as a good sign. Then he neatly separated his food and drinks from mine. "That's not my soda," he said in a panicked tone, "it's hers." The cashier looked from him to me then slowly lowered the offending can back down onto my side. He was outraged that she had even considered my stuff as part of his.

Wow, I thought Forest was cheap. This guy gave a whole new meaning to the term. He would not even pay for my single can of soda! After carrying our bags back to the car, we set off to Jason's friend's house. I had ignorantly paid for appetizers that Jason and I could share, thinking that he would do the same.

Briefly, and only for a second, I missed Richard's generosity. We arrived at the BBQ, where about 40 people were milling around in someone's garden. There was a swimming pool and a very modest home in the background, painted brown. I quickly discovered that Jason was not the kind of man I ever wanted to be with, but he was good for a laugh.

Jason ate through all of his food and more than half of mine. I chalked it up to him being hungry and decided not to be offended. As a boyfriend, it would have turned my stomach to have to be with someone so arrogantly selfish. As a friend, it was just some food. Several of Jason's friends had grabbed instruments and were making pleasing music together. I discovered many of the musicians were professional, and one guitarist had performed with Willie Nelson. This was more than your average party; it was an underground music jam session!

Jason disappeared into the house to find more food, and I fell into a natural conversation with one of the guitarists, Rick. "Been playing for quite a few years now; it's my passion. I can see that you are one passionate woman," he said to me, touching my hair. He stood with his leg on a chair, posturing, and I was flattered by the open flirting. "I saw an incredible shooting star earlier this evening." I mentioned that I did too. He held my hand, looked into my eyes, and said, "It is nice to meet you again and to meet you today. We are past souls' life connected," he said. His past life memories were obviously better than mine, but I did feel a connection looking into his soulful eyes. I could see he was a beautiful person.

Jason returned with some drinks and made a beeline to Rick and me. "I didn't get you anything, Rick, because I'm here with Katie. She's here with me. Together."

I could tell Jason felt threatened by Rick, so I tried to defuse the situation. "Rick was just telling me about his music career," I started.

"I bet he was. I bet." Jason's face started to turn red.

It was time to leave. "It's getting late, Jason. We should head back." He agreed, and we walked back to the car together. The drive back was somewhat strained. I could see that his thoughts were on Rick, and he was angry about it. The car trundled to a halt at the Lotus Retreat, and Jason's attitude changed. I realized he had gone into flirt mode.

"It was fun, Jason, thank you," I said, feeling increasingly awkward. I needed to get out of there.

"You should have danced with me," he said, the alcohol on his breath mixing with the numerous assorted foods he had taken from other people during the evening.

"That's okay...maybe next time."

Jason was not reading my body language. He leaned over to kiss me and got a mouth full of my hand.

"Woah there. I'm not looking for a hook up Jason. We're just friends, okay. Friends. I told you earlier why I came to Maui."

He did not seem upset, just confused. "Oh, you were serious. I thought you were playing hard to get."

The conversation finished with the familiar sound of a closing car door. My body had removed me from the situation. Jason sped off in his white sedan. The entire evening had made about as much sense to me as Josh shouting over a cliff to cure his continuous headache.

What a long day. And yet I had fun at the BBQ. The private concert was amazing and out of this world. This was Maui Magic in action, and I had met some cool new friends. I had to thank Jason for inviting me. *Remember to be thankful*, I reminded myself.

I collapsed on the wooden beam outside for a few moments before reentering the Bamboo Malu House. I wrote some insights in my journal:

I met a happily married couple tonight, Donny and his wife, Sada. They have known each other since high school. The message Donny kept repeating was "one love." He also said, "We are a soul family." I couldn't help noticing how happy they were together. They played music with their talented friends, and we all sang and danced. It was a joyous experience to be a part of. I asked Sada, what is the key to her good marriage? Her answer, "We are the best of friends. I want what is best for my husband; I want whatever is for his highest good, even if it means putting my needs behind his. I am a very lucky woman; he does the same for me... It really is about being each other's best friend; our love is unconditional." I left that place on a music high—a memory I will never forget.

The next day I had a wonderful massage booked and an aromatherapy session; I was looking forward to it. It is important to treat yourself well with flowers, good food, exercise, and meditation too. My thoughts flickered briefly on Richard and his masseuse girlfriend, but I pushed them away. As far as Richard was concerned, I was his teacher and he was mine. Perhaps I should really be thankful he set me free. He did me a favor.

I thought about the phone call with Thomas, and my stomach sank again. "Hoo hoo," I heard ahead of me. Looking up, a huge white owl had settled several feet above me and was looking right into my eyes. I sat frozen, unable to move while it assessed me and I considered its presence.

A coincidence? Is it possible to see a shooting star and a spirit guardian on the same evening? Perhaps that was exactly when you saw one. I felt the owl watching me and more—I felt love, safety, and a sense of destiny. Surely this was the guide the Shivas had told me that I would meet here in this magical place.

"Who indeed," I said to the owl as it flew off into the jungle. I slept soundly that night, without prescription comfort, safe in the knowledge that I was surviving the trials that had brought me here. It would have been only too easy to get romantically involved with any one of these male suitors here on Maui. I had resisted, and it was good. Still, Thomas and his many emails played on my mind. Would I be able to resist him?

Chapter 6

Mother
Maui

"*The best and most beautiful things in the world cannot be seen or even touched—they must be felt with the heart.*"

Helen Keller

Have you ever had one of those days when you have woken up and everything went wrong? That is what happened to me. The morning was as crisp as ever, but my inbox was empty. Thomas had not emailed me since the Jason phone call. I had sent him a hasty e-mail the following morning apologizing and inviting him to come to stay on Maui for a while.

Aloha Thomas,

Just wanted to apologize again for the strange call. I admit I was upset. I don't like it when I'm left waiting for a man, even though Jason and I are nothing more than friends. Don't forget about my revirginizing rule; I haven't broken it yet! It reveals such wonders.

I feel like we have connected well over the last two months, and I would love to spend some time with you in person. Why don't you come and stay on Maui? I know your business trip has run long, but surely there must be time for a few days off in between? Let me know.

Katie, XXX

Playing With Love and Beaches

Instead of finding a reply from Thomas, I re-read the email I had sent a few days ago in mild disgust. Was I too desperate? Maybe I was becoming a bit weird, Maui-fied. There was something in the air here I thought. Maybe he could see right through me. It was with a bitter taste in my mouth that I closed my laptop a fraction too hard and broke the hinge—my screen went haywire. Great!

Sita had arrived the day before, and the house was quiet from the revelry of the evening. There were no delicious bacon smells, no voices, and no screaming. Thankfully, there were also no aliens just yet, which I counted as a win while suspiciously checking the overgrowth of leaves outside of my window.

Sita was a magnificent woman, a cross between a spiritual guide, a healer, and a queen. She struck me as someone that should be emblazoned on a coin or postcard, and she seemed to understand the world in a way that few other people did. I understood Rama's infatuation with her; she was one of a kind.

My body had been up to mischief lately, brought on by pre-menopause symptoms that were ruining my recently won sleep cycles. I decided against hormone therapy but to instead go through this life change naturally with herbal remedies and healthier food. The yoga, stretching, and meditation did help. My back felt less sore, but that could have been due to the healthy smoothies Alex insisted I drink every morning. He concocted a healthy brew of omega-3s like fish oil, flax, hemp, chia seeds, fresh garlic, ginger, turmeric, and, for sweetness, a mixture of fresh fruit and coconut. He also taught me that cancer and heart disease hate a diet of 80% alkaline and 20% acidic food. He took good care of all of us and especially me.

My periods had become a nightmare, like an illness that would descend on me every month, and it had made me the least fun person at Sita's party the night before. I retired early and sober, not wanting to upset the turbulent hormones that I felt were already looking for excuses to try to kill me.

Some months I would get my period late and other times twice a month. As a younger woman, I was always regular and never had a problem. Aging might just be the challenge of a lifetime. Like a supernova star exploding, my hot flashes would take over until the final stage of life, when gravity wins. It causes the star to collapse to form a black hole, like my palpating heart, which made me feel more anxious than I should. I felt life moved quickly now; it was no longer in slow motion as it was in my youth. We all have to work through the confusion and pain of transitioning into middle age and the ability to create life taken from us while men lose their ability to maintain an erection and their hair begins to thin from fluctuating testosterone levels; they go through a type of male menopause. With my changing hormones, my periods and mood swings were similar if not worse than when I was an adolescence. My body was entering another metamorphosis, one I was not sure I welcomed—aging. No one prepares you for perimenopause or the sense of loss you feel when it happens. I said a prayer standing there in the bedroom and left for a shower. The card I drew that morning was a repeat; "Courage," it read. I needed it.

I was enjoying my hot shower for a few minutes when the temperature changed to luke warm then cold. I quickly doused myself in ice for five freezing minutes. With my thoughts on my damaged laptop and on my failed connection with Thomas, it was on days like this when I blamed Richard the most for my situation.

I imagined him fat and rich, curled up with several young women in hotels in Europe, and felt the tears well up in my eyes. I hated myself for doing it.

Today, I desperately needed my beach run to get me out of this funk and to raise my vibrations. The morning, still young, I decided to head to Baldwin, with its white, sandy beaches and light blue ocean set in stark contrast against the emerald green West Maui Mountains instantly wraps me in tranquility and reminds me to be grateful for where I am. The view is breathtaking. I park my car and begin my run on the wet sand for four miles barefoot and bikini clad to improve my all-over tan. It is a freeing experience, far better than the days of running fully dressed on asphalt in running shoes.

I have so much more energy here. After my run, I dive into the crystal clear ocean to cool down and connect with God and Mother Maui. My two hours of communion with nature to jog, do yoga and meditate alone rejuvenates me. I could easily stay there all day, but then I would get nothing done.

Although I was pre-menopausal, I was definitely experiencing a second youth. I was in the best shape of my life. The incredible weather year round makes it easy to stay in shape on Maui.

I returned to my Bamboo Malu home and joined Alex and Josh in the kitchen; Rama and Sita were sleeping in.

Alex is a psychotherapist back in New Zealand and a great source of advice here in this new life at the Lotus Farm. Sometimes it seemed like everyone that came here had retreated to rediscover real success. "I'm telling you, Alex, one of the elephant statues has completely turned around; it's eerie. I keep hearing things outside my window," Josh said over his Carl Jung book.

"Sounds like a sign," mused Alex, flipping some eggs in his traditional dress of nothing but shorts. I flopped down on the bench next to Josh and helped myself to some fresh coconut, guava, banana, and lilikoi fruit that grows plentiful on the grounds.

"There have been a few nights when I've heard noises outside my windows," I added.

"That will be the wild boars," Josh said dismissively. "I don't think they can rotate statues."

I needed some spiritual cleansing, but my Reiki appointment with Aria was in three hours' time. "My laptop is busted. Do either of you know of an IT guy that will come out here today? I need to sort it out so that I can continue to write my book."

"Oh, I can take a look at it for you," Josh said. "I'm great with computers. I'll run upstairs and have a look after breakfast."

I thanked him and continued to eat, making my way through two helpings of eggs and salad. My body needed the fuel after my morning run, and Alex could tell. He kept offering me more of whatever he was cooking. A nervous energy hung in the kitchen, born of Josh's paranoia about the statue-turning aliens and Alex's concern about me. God, I love that man. If only sweet Alex were not gay.

A Love Letter to Maui

I decided to retreat into solitude for a while but felt like I did not have the energy for a trip to the temple just yet. I had packed my journal and headed outside the back to the copse of trees where I knew I would be left in peace. The jungle around the Bamboo Malu House hummed in tuneless unison, and the silent vibrations eased the rough morning start. Josh walked by: "Goddess, may I get you a coconut refreshment?" I laughed and accepted his kind offer as I watched his young, twenty-seven-year-old, fit body climb the tree. He was barefoot and had a machete knife. He whacked at the coconut till it fell to the ground and jumped from the tree. He removed the top then got close and bowed. "I hope one night you will join me at the top of the waterfall. Think about it...there is a full moon tonight." We exchanged smiles, and I shook my finger at him for being naughty and flirting with me; I was old enough to be his mother. He left me to write. My god, I love this place.

I wrote, automatically and effortlessly, a love note to Mother Maui.

Dearest Mother Maui, it has been good to be home. Your energy is so sweet and soft. The old souls here have soothed mine, and I can feel love all around me. It is fun to play again, a youth lost and rediscovered. I am fortunate to be back in your care while going through these emotional and physical changes. I am blessed to be here in this magical place, where even bad days are full of possibility, hope, and light.

Your Aloha spirit comforts me, Mother, but I am steeped in confusion. It is easy to keep myself distant from the men of your island, but even as I pull away, my heart draws closer to another. I am in love with Thomas in some ways. A man I met briefly, a man I hardly know.

Over the last two months, he has spoken words of wisdom into my life and reignited a part of me I thought was long dead. Why, Mother, can I not control my heart? Does it long to ache? I don't know why I am so eager to be hurt again. I feel like I am betraying myself.

How ironic that I am on an island where younger men love older women, and I am getting all the attention I have ever wanted, yet I am still not satisfied. Why does my heart always drift towards someone, whether I want it to or not? Please, Mother, give me strength.

I stopped writing and sat, lost in thought. Time filled my mind, and the lack pressed hard on my heart. Yesterday morning I had received word that some of my paintings had become lost on the way here. I had to call and sort that out somehow. I felt worried about the loss and had to make time to go down to the docks to check which crates had gone awry.

Music came from inside the house, and I realized that Rama and Sita were giving a music lesson together. What harmonies! This was truly an amazing place for people with a creative spirit. I only had about a month left, and leaving was not a happy idea. I had grown to love the Woofers, the farm, and even the enigmatic Rama.

I remembered a few nights before when the Woofers did a recording with him and I got to observe and listen to Alex, Michael, and Josh hold their voices in harmony—ahhhhhh—and change the tones of their voices as instructed by Rama. This continued for twenty glorious minutes. Rama wrapped up the recording and thanked them. "Guys, I plan to use your voices in an Egyptian song I am composing. I will listen to it again when Sita returns home, and we will make love to the harmonies. We'll see how it feels.... I'll get back to you later if we decide to include it on our final record." Dear, sweet, passionate Rama—that man made me smile!

Reiki and Unblocking Energy

Early afternoon, I joined Aria at the music temple for a Reiki session overlooking the Pacific Ocean and emerald cliffs. She was bright and cheerful as always, but she looked a lot more alert than on the day I had met her. "Thanks for squeezing me in today. I could really use a pick me up," I told her.

"Oh, I'm glad you booked today. I was worried that it would be Faith again. She's a little scary."

I giggled politely, and we settled into the session. "Great...now relax...no, really relax. Stop thinking, and clear your mind. Feel your breath nice and slow." Then she sang a Hawaiian blessing, her voice beautiful, soft, gentle. She continued to guide me with her soothing words and affirmations. "Focus on the birds outside, on the nearby ocean waves...think about the white light of clarity, and allow it to dissolve your other thoughts...."

I listened intently to her voice. Aria was a master at Reiki, and my lower back had been so sore lately that I needed a healing touch. That was what Reiki was for—to channel energy from one person into another that would heal. Once I had fully relaxed, she asked me a question.

"What do you need in your life right now, Katie?"

"Money," I said without thinking. Images of the men I had dated flickered through my mind. None of them had any, that was for sure. "And love," I added.

Aria moved around me, talking gently, guiding me into a meditative state. It was a lot easier with her in charge. Rama was right; I was bad at meditation.

The feeling overtook me, and I could not tell where Aria was touching me. She rested her hands on my head, on my arms, on my heart, and on my back. I felt no pain, and the discomfort lifted in my lower body. At one point, my head felt like it was lifting off the ground. Was Aria lifting my head? I felt one hand on my arm and the other on my leg—how was this possible?—I was fading in and out. Towards the end, I felt lighter and lighter as I came out of the trance, resurfacing into a new world of positive energy. I felt refreshed again.

"That was great. Thank you. Did you lift my head near the end of the session? I had this unbelievable lightness," I said.

"Oh, I didn't touch your head," Aria mused. "That must have been your crown chakra opening up. I also opened up a blockage in your stomach—the space that represents your sexuality and creativity."

"What are you and Michael going to do today?" I asked.

"Our plans are to go wherever life takes us. We flow in the moment. Life is more fun that way...." She was a free spirit. I admired them. This was easy to do on Maui.

Visiting Sita

I left Aria feeling renewed and energized and decided to take a brisk walk to the temple, where I could do some writing and research. My laptop was still broken, so I took my phone and my notebook. On the wooden steps of the temple, a tiny grasshopper greeted me. It did not move when I stepped over it and entered the temple.

I did not think much of it at the time, but Rama told me later that night that I should have tried astral travel on my own. The grasshopper was a sign from the Universe that my spirit was primed and ready for it.

I called home and spoke to my mom and made another call to my son, Riley. He had been so busy training, but he was loving it. I was glad he was happy where he was.

After the phone calls, I sat for some time looking at the god and goddess statues. I felt an overwhelming presence that I realized was my grandmother. I knew then that she wanted me to finish my book. I also felt that she wanted me to find love. I sat suspended in her presence for some time, and my eyes watered, overcome by emotion.

I was sure that something needed to improve. Something needed to change. I felt that I had failed my mission. By falling for Thomas, had I effectively ruined the vow I had made to myself? As I sat there, I decided to seek out Sita and get her opinion on the matter. After all, it was her call that brought me here, and now I had a chance to speak with her in person.

She was deep in meditation on her own when I arrived back. On entering the music room, she opened her eyes and smiled at me. "Katie...ah yes, you would like a word." There it was, that strange intuition that hung around her like the smoke in Henry's lounge.

"Yes, please, I have..."

"Some questions you need clarity on," she said, shaking out her hands. She was wearing a decorative cotton dress in a range of purples and reds. Her silver and gold jewelry took the shape of many symbols and runes that I did not understand.

"Yes, thank you."

She gestured towards a chair and poured me a cup of tea. "Rama has already told me about your journey…I knew you would come to find me today. Oh, he's off on one of his jungle walks," she said, answering my question before I had asked it. "So what's on your mind?" She stared at me softly, full of expectation.

"I came here after I found my fiancé cheating," I started, "to rediscover myself and reconnect with what it means to be an artist and a writer. But I am struggling. I can't seem to find a way back to myself without thoughts of being with a man."

Sita nodded, setting off the many clinks and tinkering sounds of her necklaces. "Give me your hand. I am going to share something with you." Sita took my hand, and I immediately felt connected to her. She scanned my palms and closed her eyes briefly. "I am a mystic, Katie. Do you know what that is?" I shook my head. "I practice the art of human transformation through a number of various ancient practices."

"I can see that you are looking for love. But your confusion is not confusion at all. It is longing. You have learned to validate your own existence by being with a man. Instead, learn to channel that love back to yourself. This journey you have made here is not about the many men you might encounter. It is about you."

"I know all this already," I said to Sita, pain reflecting from my eyes into hers.

"Knowing something in your mind is different from accepting something in your heart. Your biggest challenge here will be to allow yourself the time to heal. To force men in your life to come second to your own needs."

She was right. As I sat there talking to her, I felt a sense of understanding. She continued, "You must know that men do not actively seek out friendship with women. They don't need it. And more, they don't know how to be friends with women. When a man tells you he only wants friendship, in his heart, he knows it is a lie. Men think differently than we do. A woman can be friends with a man, but a single man cannot be friends with a single woman."

"I think I am coming to understand this," I told her, thinking of my recent encounters and dates with the men from the island. There was hardly a moment when I did not feel sexual energy from them, even when they tried to hide it.

"A man is a logical creature, and emotions are secondary to him. He sees opportunity first and naturally puts his needs above yours."

"Even if I tell the man that I am not available?" I asked, thinking of the invitation I had extended to Thomas and his non-response.

"Men enjoy the chase. If you are single, and even sometimes when you are not, they will take that walk with you, go to dinner, hang out, whatever is needed until they see the chance to progress the relationship."

Friendships and Realities

Sita sat back on the bench, considering me. I grabbed my cup of tea to keep myself anchored. Had I really strung all those men along for my own selfish reasons? That familiar discomfort began to return to my stomach. "I have met a man that might be someone I want to be with. Even though we haven't been together, I am drawn to him."

"And have you told this man that he is just your friend?" Sita asked wisely.

"Yes," I said, "but we have flirted together in a lot of emails, and I have invited him to come to Maui to see me in person."

"Then don't fool yourself, Katie. You are romantically interested in this man, despite your vows and despite what you say."

I finished my tea in one gulp. It nearly spilled out of my mouth, there was so much of it. "You have set yourself up for a relationship under the guise of friendship. It is too late for you now. You have invited him here, and so the chase begins. If he feels a strong connection to you, he will come. Then you owe him a shot."

Sita was right. The single male friends I spent time with wanted more from me, while in fact I was planning to see if Thomas was the man of my romantic dreams. I had been priming him all this time for the eventual meeting. I clutched at my heart.

"Yes, pain. Ache. That is there because you are not yet over the trauma experienced with your ex, Richard."

I looked up at her and saw that she was smiling. "Katie, you know that the best thing for you right now is to recover from your emotional pain. If you truly love this man, you owe it to him too. Otherwise, your heart will never heal completely, and it will impact what you have together. You know, deep down, that you are not ready for him yet."

"Well, I don't think he is coming anyway. I made him angry with me the other night."

Sita gave me a knowing look then stretched and rose off the bench. "It's just about time for my evening dip in the ocean. Care to join me?"

"Ah, no thank you, I told Faith I would find her and have an early dinner with her tonight." My thoughts swirled inside me. Sita gave me a hug goodbye and taught me the proper way to hug is heart to heart, the left side of my chest against hers.

The Struggle for Faith

I stumbled out of the music room, barely looking where I was going, and ran straight into blue-faced Rama. "The vibrations are strong with you today, Katie," he said as he strutted by, wild-eyed and beaming.

"Have you seen Faith?" I asked.

"She was upstairs in her room the last time we spoke...which was yesterday."

"Thanks," I said, more bemused than he was. I needed a friend. I made my way up the bamboo staircase and knocked tentatively on Faith's door.

"I don't want any," she called back.

"It's me...Katie," I whispered through the door. "I brought you some food." A second later the door jolted open, a chain keeping me from her.

The door closed then was latched open again. I slipped inside. "Your room has a chain lock?" I asked, wishing mine did too. On more than one occasion, I had the overwhelming sensation someone was in my room with me.

Faith was laid back and had a deep respect for nature. She was also artistic and different. Hawaiians believe that everything and everyone is connected in the grand circle of life. Every person can positively impact another, if they choose. Intelligence was just not as important as connection. It made sense to me.

Since arriving at the Lotus Retreat and Farm, everyone I had encountered lived the Aloha spirit. They were all individual miracles in my life. From Rama's wild and free spirit to Sita's mystery, Alex's nurturing support, Aria's healing, and Josh's adorable charm, they had all touched me in a way that made my life better. Faith had done the same with her total acceptance of who she was. She never apologized for it and always said what was on her mind.

Faith's bedroom was fancier than mine, decked out in red instead of my purple and with more flags and ornaments dotted around the room. A large, ornate cloth hung over her four poster bed. I plopped myself down into a red beanbag chair, and Faith sat down next to me on a green couch. I told her about Sita and how

I felt about the meeting.

"That woman has great karma, and Rama is a groovy cat," she said to me, scrolling through her tablet. "You should pay attention to what she says. Life is about finding our way to success, not finding our way to more men. Men are everywhere. They all want sex and think that we are as desperate for it as they are. I promise you, the attention isn't going to vanish either way. You're thinking about Thomas now, aren't you?" Faith said to me, reaching for her nail polish.

"I can't help it. He hasn't emailed me since I called him Jason. I really thought there was something between us."

"Well, that's email for you. It's easier getting to know a man in person. That way you can really tell if there is chemistry."

Faith started to paint her toe nails, and I made myself comfortable on the beanbag, leaning back and staring at her ceiling. "True, and even then, chemistry may not be enough. That's what happened with my second fiancé Nathan. Several years after I divorced Sam, I met this amazing man that I was instantly attracted to."

"Yeah? What happened?"

The leaves outside rustled as night began to descend on the Bamboo Malu House. "The sex was mind blowing, but it was a toxic relationship. We dated for seven years, and it was a whirlwind of passion. I mean regular massages, we cooked for each other, and he was kind and loved my son, Riley. There were a lot of ups and downs. Eventually it felt like my head was spinning and my stomach was churning. I had to get off the ride," I told her.

"Sounds tough. Why did it end?"

I considered the question carefully. "I was an addiction to him, and he was an addiction to me. He needed so much attention, and his mood swings were unbearable. I ended the relationship when he needed to move for work and refused to marry me. He could not commit, and I could not continue being his crutch...so it ended."

"You have terrible luck with men," Faith said, lightening the mood.

"Don't I know it! I still remember praying to God and begging him to send me a healthy man to provide for me and my son. Imagine that! Instead of praying for myself and God to provide! That was when I first saw the writing on the wall. The message came through loud and clear—I needed to put my trust in myself, in God, not in another man."

"A few years later I met Richard. I really thought he was the one, my knight in shining armor, the last man I was intimate and faithful to for the past seven years before arriving on Maui," I mused.

"Well, he wasn't. And now that's finished, and you are better off for it. Sita is right. You need to focus on yourself more. All of these men are confusing you. They are confusing me! It's just as well that this Thomas character has stopped emailing you."

I knew that Faith was trying to help, but I still felt sad about it. I really liked Thomas. I liked the words he sent to me and could still smell that oak polish and herbal scent that had attracted me that day at the airport. The man sold women's shoes, for crying out loud. Could there be a more attractive profession?

I left Faith's room feeling resolute that I would stick to my vows and focus on myself. Whether Thomas was gone or not, I would continue the healing process. There was still a lot of life to live, and I wanted it all. No man was ever going to prevent me from reaching my full potential ever again. With that, I started to fall into a dreamless sleep.

"Blink" went my inbox.

Chapter 7

Dancing With Yourself

"If you aren't living on the edge,
you are taking up too much space."

Anonymous

Aloha Katie,

Sorry about not getting back to you sooner. There was a crisis with our fall line of kicks, and I had to convince a very reluctant designer to sign a new contract for less money. I managed to close the deal though, so we are in the aftermath of the struggle.

How have things been on Maui?

I think of you there, lying on a golden beach in the sun without a care in the world. I would love to join you, but I still have a few things to wrap up here first. My first course of action will be to get Rachel Ling, a woman with the most incredible poker face, to sign off on our design proofs. Wish me luck—she has a reputation for being a ferocious adversary for buyers everywhere.

Still dreaming of you...Thomas x

The Possibility of Ecstatic Love

My eyes fluttered open as I read the email once, twice, then a third time. Once I was satisfied that it was positive, a new feeling flooded into my heart. So he had not vanished after all. I still had a chance with this man.

I fell asleep that night and woke with a jolt that morning. I read the email again a few times just to be sure before I headed down the hallway to the card table en route to the communal bathroom. Thomas was still interested, and he sounded like he really wanted to join me. The only thing separating us was an uncooperative woman named Rachel.

As I walked, I did not even hear the musical instruments heating up the floor below me. I was in a mist of thoughts, daydreaming about my future honeymoon with the very impressive Thomas. I felt he would love me like no one had ever loved me before.

I came to the little circular table and prepared myself for the card of the day. I had been picking so many "clarity"' and "courage" cards that I thought the deck had been fixed. Somewhere the divine goddess was trying to tell me something. I reached out and picked another card. "Love," it said. Was this a sign?

Surely it was not a cosmic coincidence that Thomas had emailed me for the first time in ages on that same day that I picked the love card. Smiling to myself, I hurried through my morning routine in the shower and bustled back to the room, where I unloaded my toiletries before heading down to the kitchen below.

That night I would write a powerful email to Thomas to strengthen our bond together. I took the last few wooden stairs at a jump, my spirits high. "Aloha, guys," I announced, grabbing the first piece of toast I could see.

Sita sat pensively in her dark navy blue and white dress, sipping a cup of tea next to the kitchen window. "Are you joining us for some ecstatic dancing this morning, Katie?" she asked me, not taking her eyes away from the direct sunlight.

I had no idea what it was, but it sounded fun—and I was in a brave mood. "Absolutely, count me in. Sounds great," I said between crunches.

Alex and Josh traded knowing looks. "She has no idea what that is, Sita," Alex remarked.

"Just as well," Sita mused. "It's better to experience it first than to be scared off by descriptions."

I stopped chewing briefly and looked around the table. I could tell that ecstatic dancing was not a common practice. "Why are we doing it? What's wrong?" I asked.

It was Rama's turn to speak. "Strange vibrations in the air. We have been feeling a tension in the house for the last few days. We thought a good ecstatic dancing session would sweat it out."

"Don't worry, Katie. I'll be there to guide you through it." Josh winked before he looked around the room suspiciously. "We could all do with an aura cleanse."

After breakfast, Rama, Sita, Alex, Josh, and Aria reconvened in the music room. For the first time, I noticed a tablet of text on the wall. *"You can merge with God. Communing with nature is good for the soul. To heal is to make whole. Faith healing is to be in a state of love continuously. Hands-on faith healing is real. There is a cure for cancer. Seek miracles, and miracles will seek you. Time travel is possible. Interdimensional communication is easy,"* it read.

"Where is Faith?" I asked Aria as she lined up next to me.

"She won't come out of her room. Says she needs time alone." She shrugged.

I wondered why she did not say anything to me the night before when I visited. Then again, I was preoccupied with my own troubles. I made a mental note to try to help her overcome whatever was keeping her locked inside that room.

"A quick review," announced Sita as Rama turned on some melodic sounds, "for the new among us..." She flashed her eyes at me, and I stood, nervous and waiting for instructions. "Your dance space is a conscious space; keep it to yourself. Be aware of the dancers around you, and do not enter their private revelry. And please...no funny business."

I could have sworn she looked at Josh for a moment before the James Brown song "I Feel Good" got louder. Immediately, dancing broke out in all forms. Aria was spinning around in circles, Rama was grabbing at something in the air, Alex had gone into some kind of silent tribal chant with eyes closed, and Josh was rolling around on the ground, shaking it off.

Sita looked like she was feeling the air around her. I stood frozen, gently swaying back and forth. I had no idea what I was doing, and I felt like a repressed conservative because of it. "Do what you feel, Katie. No one is here to judge you. This is how you open yourself back up and seize liberation back from the ether," said Sita in a sing-song voice as she floated by.

I closed my eyes, trying not to be aware of my stiffness and self-consciousness. Why was this so hard for me? Everyone else looked spectacular. The music kept building, going faster and faster as the thirty-minute session progressed. Eventually, I was jumping, which I felt a lot more comfortable with because everyone else had launched into leaps naturally.

We worked up a good sweat, and I waved my arms around freely. It felt wonderful, yet I could not let go of myself. What was my problem? Alex and Josh were my problems. I did not want to look foolish in front of these attractive men. A little upset that I had been forced to pretend some, the music suddenly stopped.

"Awesome session, guys!" called Alex, giving Rama a high five. They grabbed some towels on the side of the music room bench and cleared out after that. Everyone but Josh. I found myself drying off my neck when I felt his eyes skating over my body. There was an imposing sexual energy about him despite his love for marijuana and conspiracy theories.

When I turned to leave the room, there he was. In one step, he was right up against me. "You have some rocking moves, Katie," he said, glistening from his own tribal expressions.

My heart rate increased as he reached out and curled my hair in his fingers. "Ah, thanks, Josh...I felt quite exposed." I could feel his breath touch my face.

"You and I should dance together sometime...or maybe go for a dip at the waterfall. Remember the full moon I spoke about earlier?" he said, his light eyes filled with promises and insinuations. "Great place for a proposal. I mean, I'd like to marry a smoking hot woman like you. Why haven't you and I been on a date yet?" he asked casually as I looked up at his handsome, youthful face. He had two days' worth of stubble.

"You know why I'm here, Josh. Just to have fun...you, my darling, are a little young for me, but I am really flattered," I said, thinking about Sita's words.

"Right," Josh said, still smiling, "I have mad respect for that, I do. If you ever change your mind though, we could have fun together, a life together, whatever...I give great massages..." He let go of my hair and wandered back to the kitchen. "Katie, don't forget that you are a hot and fiery woman. I've always liked artistic girls like you." He winked at me as he went. Sweet, young Josh. I will always remember him for his daily compliments reminding me that I was so hot I was on fire; He had a proclivity for associating words of heat and flame with beauty. Surely goddess Pele must have inspired him to play with fire.

Hanging Out With the Woofers

I felt extremely hot, in a way that had nothing to do with the dancing I had just enjoyed. I returned to my room and wondered what I should do with the rest of my morning. Perhaps I would visit Faith and find out what was going on with her. I was in a really good mood though. Maybe it would be better to use the positive energy to write.

Aria suddenly poked her head in through the window outside, where she stood on the wraparound lanai, and I nearly flung the book I was holding at her. "Katie!" she almost shouted. "Properly good dance this morning, hey! I feel brilliant—alive, you know! The Woofers and I are going fishing down at the beach. Want to come with?" I certainly did, so I met them outside with a little bag packed.

As we set off, Aria looked down at my pants and frowned. "You gotta take off your shoes and socks and roll up those pants for this hike. I can see you need to reconnect with nature." Alex was out front chatting expressively with Josh, who was still occasionally shooting me sexually charged looks.

"I haven't...shaved my legs..." I said as she stared back at me, expectation in her eyes.

"I haven't either," she said, gesturing to her legs. "Who cares? It's about feeling nature. Your hair will help you do that!" I thought about it for a moment and then caved, packing my shoes and socks into my bag and rolling up my pants. I wished I had thought to shave.

We hiked down the jungle path, passed the temples, and continued down the long, winding dirt path to the beach below the cliffs. It did feel amazing. "You've picked up some hitchhikers," Alex said to me as he streaked off into the sea for a dip. I looked down, and there were little green plant heads all over my pants, and some even managed to stick to the hair on my legs. I was so embarrassed!

It was a lovely morning that transitioned effortlessly into an epic afternoon. We collected mussels from the rock pools, and the boys fished, although no one caught anything. I could tell that line fishing without a pole was a difficult way to catch a fish.

Michael came down and met Aria. I watched the love exchange between the two. What beautiful souls. They stared deep into each other's eyes.

"How long have you lived on the Lotus Farm?" I asked Michael.

"Uh what?" he said, his eyes fixed on Aria.

"How long have you lived at the Retreat?" I pressed again.

He could not take his eyes off Aria. "Uh, I don't know," he replied in a soft, dreamy voice. He was in a love trance, shutting out the world. Aria smiled broadly, noticing Michael could not speak, her eyes penetrating his. I smiled too and left the lovebirds alone.

Alex and Josh, were wading in the pools. I found a shady spot and began writing in my journal:

Aria and Michael are drug free and eat very healthy. This woman is a great reiki master; I can attest from personal experience. She is adorable and sweet. The other day she gave a reiki session to a frog that she claimed looked lifeless for days at our pond. She brought it back to life, and it hopped away. Aria always reminds me, "Nourishing equals encouraging" and "Bare feet touching the land and grass infuses healing energy."

On the hike down to the beach, there was a lot of mud, and she stepped in a big pile of wild boar poop...ick. There was one reason I preferred to wear shoes on my hikes to the beach. She said it was squishy between her toes and warm. I could tell she wanted to be first in the ocean to wash her feet, so she gently pushed her way to the front.

Aria shared with me that before she came to reside at the Lotus Farm as one of the Woofers, Michael would sing a song, a prayer he created, knowing with faith that his beloved would hear it across the open sea an invitation to come to join him. Aria

133

answered the call. Rama had told me love brings people to Maui and specifically to their land. I believe it and have witnessed several love connections. Aria and Michael are my youngest role models on love.

Michael is sweet and quiet and keeps to himself except when it comes to Aria. He wants to live off the land and chooses not to participate in our group breakfasts or dinners. He is always barefoot, even when he plays soccer and even when he jogs around downtown Paia. He is handsome, tan, and lean with no body fat. He is high energy.

Aria taught me that breathing is so important. It is another food source for your body. I reconnected to the land, to this life force, this mana (energy) of Hawaii—the 'HA' breath of life. I love exercising and walking the grounds at the Lotus Farm. I touch the trees daily and think about the lessons I have learned here and the book I'm trying to write. I paused from my writing. I teared up then and continued. I love feeling the energy of the trees, the dirt and grass beneath my bare feet. I think of the pure love and innocence of the young. No money, yet they don't care. They are just so in love and have a big vision for each other and their lives.

The Sidewalk Musician

Aria and I decided to head into town to pick up some groceries for the Bamboo Malu House. Rama had insisted that Alex cook up all the fresh organic tomatoes so that they would heighten the psychic vibrations at the breakfast plate reading that morning. I could not imagine what mine would have said, other than "not hungry anymore." I giggled to myself.

There was an amazing palm tree with a blue bench underneath it as we pulled into the parking lot in my economy car. "Would you mind if I stayed here and wrote a little more?" I asked Aria, feeling inspired.

"Not at all. I won't be long. Happy writing!" she said, scurrying off to Mana Foods.

I begin to write:

All women are goddesses...the men in Haiku and Paia say this a lot. The men clasp their hands in prayer position and sometimes even do a little bow for the lady. It is so adorable. They also frequently use words like brother and sister. Like Brother Alex. I love it. One day I was having car issues and this man, called out to me, "Having trouble sistah? You need any help?" he says in his singsong voice.

A musician friend of mine told me a funny story. He was hired to perform on a private tantra boat trip. He played his Hawaiian music while people around him were smoking pot, beating their bongo drums and shaking their tambourines. Some were naked or in their bathing suits. It was whale watching season, and some of the people were mooing and moaning to imitate the whales. The whales got close to the boat. The passengers got more and more excited and continued communicating in whale language. They were all leaning over the edge of the boat to get a closer look. My friend said all he could see was a sea of asses staring him in the face. He said it was the strangest gig he ever played and one he will never forget. He said the people were so nice, respectable, and sweet to him.

Across from the blue bench behind me was a sugarcane field, just beautiful. I should grab a seat there. Maybe it was time to write back to Thomas. I caught movement in my peripheral vision and decided to stay in my car. A man in his early forties, wearing obviously discarded clothes that were torn in places, was moving around my vehicle. He looked dazed. One of Paia's homeless. My window was rolled down, and my guard went up. Out of all the cars in the parking lot, he had to lean on mine; then he started smoking his cigarette. I wanted to lock my door and roll up my window, but he would hear the click. *He looks harmless enough*, I told myself. *I don't want to draw attention.*

There are homeless people in Paia—some are down on their luck or mentally ill, while others are addicts. I could not tell which one he was. He had arranged his toothless grin into what he believed was a friendly smile. I tried hard not to stare at the solitary tooth that jutted out of his lower jaw.

Quietly, I hoped he would leave me alone. "Oh my god, so sorry. I didn't see you sitting there," he said to me in a gravelly voice. He removed his backside from my car and turned to half face me. "Really, sorry I touched your car. I didn't mean nothing by it," he said, his curious smile reaching.

"It's fine," I said back, trying not to make eye contact.

"How about a quarter?" he asked firmly.

I looked up—he was wearing a pair of sunglasses that had seen better days. One lens was so cracked and scratched I wondered how he could see at all.

"Sorry, I don't carry cash on me."

"Oh, that's okay. I understand. A bum like me pestering you for change. You're probably doing something important," he continued.

He was genuinely nice, not what I had expected. We chatted together for a few minutes, and each time I tried to imply that I could no longer talk, he effortlessly ignored me. I found out that he had once been a musician but had fallen on hard times. He was a songwriter who played the bass guitar. Something stirred inside me, my own dreams. I admitted to him I had just moved to the island. After 10 minutes, I finally said, "I'm sorry, but I actually am doing work here. I am waiting for my girlfriend to return from shopping; she will be here any minute now. I'm sorry. It was nice meeting you."

He did not listen to my request in the slightest. Then he started to ramble about his mom and gay sister. I listened politely. He told me that his mom and sister had a falling out when she came out of the closet. But he always knew the truth about his sister and still loved her. He told me his name was Larry, and he asked me for my name.

"Are you a lesbian? No biggie. I just don't know if you like guys or girls. Either way is cool with me...." I didn't answer his question. I wanted him to go away.

"Hey, what happened to your eye?" I asked.

"It was stupid. An accident. I told my friend a joke, and he thought it was so funny. He laughed so hard and shoved me out of the way and said, 'Get out of town; that is hilarious.' I fell over and hit my face on the blacktop."

"Wow, that must be some kind of joke." I was now curious. "Can you tell me the joke?"

"Yeah sure, it goes like this...why won't the orangutans play poker with the apes anymore?"

"Why?"

"Because they are a bunch of cheetahs."

I laughed and said, "That is a stupid joke, but I love it."

"That is why I asked you for change...because look at my face...I can't go to work like this. I had a job lined up too," he said.

Larry pointed to his friend who had pushed him over in the parking lot. They looked like normal guys. Larry seemed slightly stoned or drunk but harmless. I tried to end our conversation politely and told him once again, "Larry, I'm sorry, but I have work to do...."

"Just so you know, me and my friends have your back if you ever needed us. We are always in town."

I could tell this man needed love, and I was overflowing with good feelings from the jungle. "Hey, how can you see out of those glasses with that lens all scratched up? Why don't you take these sunglasses instead? That way you will see better. You can't be a bass player without a cool pair of shades."

He was very thankful. "Wow, how cool of you. Are you sure? I don't know if they will fit my big head!"

"Don't worry; they stretch. I have a big head too. Try them on." He did, and they fit him snugly. When he removed his glasses, I saw that his eye was worse than I thought; it was bruised and deeply scratched. He seemed moved almost to tears. He was touched about the sunglasses, I could tell.

"Okay, thank you for the sunglasses. It's really nice of you." He sounded a little choked up. Finally, he walked away.

Five minutes later he came back to my car just as I was wrapping up my last e-mail. I shut the computer off.

"Hey, sorry to bother you again, but I want to sing a song I just wrote for you. Here it goes...Katie, I love you, I love you, oh Katie, you are so beautiful, I love you still..." He stopped, beaming at me, and said, "I'm not finished yet, but I will finish it one day, and it will be a hit song on the radio. And it's because you inspired it."

It was kind of sweet, and I was glad I had made him happy. I smiled at him and clapped my hands in gratitude. "Mahalo, Larry, that was a beautiful start to a heartwarming song. I will never forget you." And I meant it.

"Goodbye, Katie, and thanks for the sunglasses."

Aria returned to the car, and in twenty minutes, we rolled into the Lotus Farm. We got out of the car and walked straight into Jason, who had been waiting for me outside the Bamboo Malu House.

Jason Comes Calling

"Katie! Hey! I wanted to see you!" He was wearing a light blue and white sleeveless shirt, and his huge muscles were spilling everywhere. I had taken to blowing him off since our date disaster, but he was persistent, I will give him that.

I knew why he had come. I knew what he wanted from me. Jason was a lot of things—subtle was not one of them. Had I driven him to this kind of blatant display of engagement? I thought about Thomas and hardened my resolve.

He played with my hair and stroked my arm. Dammit, I was attracted to him. "You and I would make a good looking couple wouldn't you say?" he asked, whispering in my ear. The smell of his cologne was pleasant and masculine. "I'm going out of town soon," he started. *Here we go....*

I cut him off. "I'm not ready to be in an intimate relationship Jason. I am here to focus on myself...you know that." He thought about it for a moment and then smiled. I could see that this was a man who enjoyed the chase. Pity he would never catch me.

"Okay Katie, how about we go out to dinner, as friends." He asked. I hesitated, then accepted.

That evening was something special, even for Jason, who I could see was turning on the charm and pulling out all of the tricks he could think of. I felt like a queen, I am not going to lie. He opened my car door, pulled out my chair for me, and even bought me a rose from a passing flower seller. I giggled like a schoolgirl when he put it in my hair.

Over dinner, I learned more about Jason and his financial situation. He was in the same boat as me—he had to earn a lot more money, and fast. I felt more comfortable now with paying for my meal and anticipated it when the bill finally came. Jason had plowed through two bottles of wine and was giving me bedroom eyes.

As I reached for the bill, he lunged for it, knocking a glass of red wine into my lap. "Oh, I'm so sorry, babe, but I will get this. No, it's for me to get. I will get this one. Really. I will," he slathered at me. At least he had spotted the error of his previous ways. He opened his eyes a little wider to take in the bill amount. "Maybe not..." he said, exhaling hard.

Smelling of red wine and with my right leg sporting a lovely red patch, I laughed. "Jason, it's okay. I'll pay my way. We're friends," I repeated, trying to ignore Sita's voice in my memory that men cannot be friends with a woman. Jason was definitely trying to leap over the friend zone.

"Nonsense. I invited you, didn't I?" he insisted. "You have such beautiful eyes, Katie, did you know? I could swim in them." The ocean rolled by the restaurant, covered in the darkness of the evening.

We got into the car a short while later after I insisted on driving us back. Jason was lost in the chase, and I felt guilty about it. What would Thomas think? "Katie...Katie? Would you come to a drum session with me sometime? I think you would like it...."

Again, I was trapped. The moment I parked the car, Jason leaned in and planted a soggy, wet kiss on my mouth. It took me completely by surprise. I pushed him back, my heart beating harder. "What's wrong?" he asked, upset.

"I know you are into me, Jason, but I would prefer it if we were just friends. The thing is...I'm not ready," I blurted, furious with myself. What was wrong with me? Why couldn't I tell him I wasn't interested?

Jason was not happy. He left, complaining that he had to pay for dinner, forgetting that I had paid my way. He was fun to hang out with, but boy, could that man party. I got upstairs and cried for a while. "Love" my card said. It was propped against my laptop screen. I knew that my hormones were getting to me.

To calm down, I folded my legs and straightened out my spine. Meditation. That would be the thing I would feel proud about conquering today. I breathed deeply and sank into a kind of melodic trance. There was a crack outside, and my head whipped around. Oh god. One of my elephant statues was facing the wrong way. Was it the aliens?

Rama and Josh were always talking about them like they existed. Like at any moment I would look out of my window and see a small green man with giant eyes. I breathed again. There was no such thing as aliens. On the "no aliens" mantra, I managed to ignore the scraping sounds outside.

Naked Drumming at the Beach

For the first time since I had arrived at the Lotus Retreat, I had let go of my thoughts and managed to meditate for a good 15 minutes. It was not a record, but it was a start. Afterwards, I decided to go to Jason's Sunday drum circle the next day. I was curious for a new adventure. I had to explain to him that I was possibly in love with another man and that we would never be together like that.

I had to face the possibility that I would lose him as a friend because of the truth. The day passed by in restful quiet as I wrote in the temple and practiced my newfound meditation skills. It was late afternoon, and I drove myself to Little Beach to meet Jason. I could see the sunset fires in the distance and ran into Crystal, one of the Woofers.

She was almost completely naked. As I got out of my car, she waved at me, her breasts jumping around her chest enthusiastically. All she was wearing was a scarf around her middle. It hid nothing, and I wondered why she was wearing it. "Katie! Great to see you here! I didn't think a naked drumming circle was your thing!"

I looked around, and sure enough, most of the people milling around the Little Beach entrance were in various stages of nakedness. The air smelled of ocean and weed. Crystal was very clearly stoned, as were others. "Take it off. Let it all hang out. Don't be timid. Celebrate your beautiful body!" she said to me from the entrance, sipping on a bottle of something.

I peeked over the dune, and there was Jason, surrounded by naked women. How foolish I had been! Jason didn't care about Thomas or the fact that I blew him off. I was just another game to him. I watched for a few minutes as Jason, in all of his naked glory, danced around the bonfire. There were several naked people drumming a rhythmical beat.

I was open minded, but I did not want my brains to fall out. This was not for me, but what a story to tell! I will never forget those candid gyrations of a naked, intoxicated Jason. This was one lady he would not add to his naked harem of dancers.

Gross National Happiness (GNH)

Back at the Bamboo Malu House that evening, Sita said goodbye to me. She was off to see the queen of Bhutan. Rama looked sad to see her go. She would leave the next day for a one-week trip. She gave me a warm hug and said I would be welcome to live at the Bamboo Malu House for another three months in the future, if that was what I wanted. She also told me to make sure that the new place I moved to had a good sense of energy to boost my creative ability. Sita said that during my time at the Lotus Retreat, she noticed I learned to be sensitive and in harmony with the land. She observed me blossom into a beautiful flower, and she could see the positive changes in me. I was reenergized and happy.

"People come and go here, so I have learned to let go," she told me. "Good people come, and we touch and unite in the heart. But journeys often lead people away, so I prefer to see them off with joy." Sita is friends with the queen of Bhutan and other spiritual masters, which I find incredible.

Bhutan does not measure their wealth by the world standard of gross domestic product (GDP). Instead, it measures its wealth in terms of gross national happiness, or GNH. They are tied and connected to the land to find happiness, even though they are one of the poorest countries in the world, according to Western terms and GDP.

Gross national happiness—what an inspiring way to measure the success of a place. Measuring prosperity through formal principles, GNH, and the spiritual, physical, social, and environmental health of its citizens and natural environment makes a lot of sense—more sense than placing money on a pedestal, like once you have it, happiness is the inevitable result. That is just not the case.

Thakur Singh Powdyel, Bhutan's Minister of Education, has become one of the most eloquent spokespeople for GNH. He says, "We believe you cannot have a prosperous nation in the long run that does not conserve its natural environment or take care of the wellbeing of its people, which is being borne out by what is happening to the outside world. GNH is an aspiration, a set of guiding principles through which we are navigating our path towards a sustainable and equitable society. We believe the world needs to do the same before it is too late."

Rama offered me another heart reading. I gladly accepted. He placed his hand between my breasts. We sat face to face. He allowed himself time for his own circulatory system to fall into the same steady rhythm as mine until oneness overcame us. At first, Rama was disappointed because in his interpretation, it would be much longer than six months, possibly even a couple years, before he saw me with a good man that was meant for me. He did see something wonderful however—"the elegance of love"—a vision of a lady standing proudly on her own two feet, happy with herself, born from a renewed internal strength.

"That's a good sign," he told me. "For when a woman loves herself and is not in need of a man, you can be sure that the perfect lover is on his way to her."

Chapter 8

Dinner With Faith

"We keep moving forward, opening new doors, and doing new things, because we're curious and curiosity keeps leading us down new paths."

Walt Disney

My time at Rama and Sita's Lotus Retreat and Farm was almost over. With only two weeks remaining, I decided to ask Faith to dinner to chat about her problems. From what I could tell, it seemed to revolve around her impatience with her music career, a lack of financial support from her family, and the absence of a good man in her life. I could relate.

Getting to Know Faith

Faith chose Casanova Italian Restaurant, where live music would be playing. It was a festive place, upcountry in historic Makawao. It was one of my favorite Italian bistros on the island. "I'm not much in the mood for food," remarked Faith as we were seated at our table.

"What do you feel like then?" I asked, always willing to indulge her flights of fancy.

"How about dessert and shots?" she said, smoothing out the menu.

"Sounds glorious. I haven't had a good dessert for dinner in way too long," I said.

We decided to each enjoy a hot chocolate lava brownie with ice-cream for dinner. They came with sparklers, firing off white glittering lights in every direction. "I told them it was your birthday," Faith said, thrilled by the display.

"It's not though," I said quizzically, in wonder of her spontaneous lust for fun.

"The sparklers disagree."

Then the shots started. Faith ordered several rounds, and they came in all colors. By my third shot, I waited for Faith to turn away so that I could feed the next one to the plant behind me. She was on a mission. I knew it was time to leave when the hiccupping started. They flew out of Faith's mouth, jerking her entire body this way and that.

I placed an order to go, fettuccine portofino and foccia bread. We paid the bill and we retired to the car, in good spirits. "No I'll drive, really," I said.

Faith threw up her hands: "Sober is my middle name." I had reservations about driving in the same car as Faith, who had a notorious reputation in any vehicle even when she was sober. She acquiesced, and I took the wheel.

We pulled into the dirt road that led to the farm and parked the car. Finally, she shared more story about her life. "I was married once before and gave birth to a beautiful baby boy eight years ago to the day. We named him John...he died eighteen days later. I remember during my pregnancy feeling Baby John kicking and moving up until the eighth month of pregnancy. Then I knew something was wrong. I was getting really big; even my doctors noticed. In the end, I had a caesarean. When they cut into my belly, my amniotic fluid sprayed out, and all I remember was how quickly they took my baby out of the room. They would not let me see him. I knew something was seriously wrong. He was born with a rare condition, Spinal Muscular Atrophy Type 1. My husband and I were both missing a certain chromosome, leaving our baby paralyzed at seven pounds. No muscles worked; he had to have tubes down his throat. God, it was awful. He couldn't breathe on his own and was placed in an incubator. He was starving; he wasn't getting all the fluids he needed. The doctors tested him over and over, prodding and poking him. He made no sound; he could not yell or scream. He only made facial expressions. His forehead would wrinkle up, and tears rolled down his eyes."

"Finally, the doctor's suggested they take the tubes out and cut a hole in his throat so that he could breathe on his own. The chances of survival were not good. My husband and I decided that this was not the life we wanted for our son; he would not live long and would be paralyzed. We took him off the life-support machine and placed him on portable oxygen. We called our closest friends and family. They met us at the hospital for his last day on earth. I will never forget it; it was a beautiful, sunny morning with bright blue skies. It was Baby John's first time outdoors and off the machines. My husband and I took turns holding him close, snuggling and kissing him. The sun was warm on his soft skin. It was time to remove the tubes, and as we did, three orange monarch butterflies fluttered by us and formed their own circle flying upwards and away. I was the one who got to hold Baby John and feel his last breath. I actually felt his spirit leave his fragile body. We all grieved together on the lawn."

It was the first time I saw Faith cry.

"Faith, I am so sorry you lived through that. What a terrible loss." My eyes watered as I felt her sadness.

I felt a strong sense that her baby was with us as she re-experienced it. She sniffed. I gave her a napkin, and she wiped the tears from her eyes. She pulled herself together and continued, "I saw a few monarch butterflies around me earlier today. They were dancing and fluttering around, and it reminded me that my baby is still near. Orange monarch butterflies are a sign from John. When my baby died, I wanted to die and thought about driving off a cliff but couldn't bring myself to do it. I was put on antidepressants, and after six months, I decided to kick them, and that was when I got into yoga and started writing my music again."

She had been working on moving to Maui just like me for the last five years. She and her husband divorced almost a year after their baby's death. She learned to let go of material things, in order to keep her life simple. She had come across the same Luscious Life Tour video that brought me to Sita and brought us together as friends.

There were two new people outside on the wooden bench. I hugged Faith good night in a long heart to heart embrace—she wanted to be alone. "Are you sure?" I asked.

"Yes, I will be okay, really.... It is always painful this time of year. Yet as time passes, the experience becomes a little more bearable. I'm glad to be here at the Lotus Retreat...."

I introduced myself to the new arrivals, and we fell into a natural conversation.

Angelina was tall and thin, 24 years old, and an artist like me. With dark brown curly hair and rosy cheeks, I could see the man next to her was interested. His name was Hai, a new guest joining us from Asia. Short and fashion conscious, his sheet of black hair was appealing. He clipped it back into a masculine bun.

"I've lived on Maui my whole life, and this is the weekend I lose my virginity," Angelina openly shared with us.

"Oh?" I asked. "Who is the lucky man?"

"Not sure yet, but the gods will bring me someone, I'm sure," she added, beaming. I tried not to look confused but did a bad job of it. "I can see you think it's strange, but I want to decide when and where."

"I think it's brave," added Hai, his eyes full of desire.

Of course you would, I thought. *You want to take advantage!* "Well, I consider myself a born again virgin," I said. "Sex complicates things. If it was me, I would wait as long as possible. Men can be tricky," I confessed, standing to take my leave. This was too much weirdness for me in one night.

"Good to have you here, Hai. I'm sure we'll become good friends. As for you, young lady," I said, shooting Angelina a warning look, "try not to rush into anything you will regret." I stomped back up the stairs, dizzy from the declarations that younger women made. Faith did not need a man to be happy, and Angelina was willing to just give her virginity away.

But then, this was Maui, and the spirits of sexuality were strong here. I reaffirmed my commitment to being revirginized and climbed into bed that night, my heart renewed. I thought about the sacredness of love and relationships as I wrote in my journal:

I spoke to a man in his late 30s who was born and raised in India. He relocated to the USA fifteen years ago. I told him I knew many Indian couples who had prearranged marriages, and they seem happily married. He agreed that many do last. He is Americanized himself and works for Facebook. His view on why there are so many divorces in Western society is that we have too many choices. We are an attention deficit society. We can't make up our minds. There was always something better around the corner or something (someone) else to try. It is hard for people to want to commit.

Paul, a wiser older man, lost his wife to cancer. They had been happily married for over forty-five years. He is new to the dating scene and doesn't like it. He admits, things have changed a great deal since he was single. His observation is that young people nowadays, change partners as often as they change their underwear. I asked him what the secret was to his long, happy marriage. His answer was that they both took their wedding vows seriously. It was a lot of work sometimes, but humor and laughter got them through most of life's situations. They kept their relationship happy and made each other laugh and they were the best of friends.

Harley and Dianne have been together as a married couple for forty years. It is his second marriage and her first. They are happy and still madly in love. He is 80, and she 70. They look much younger than their biological ages. I asked them their secret to aging well. They stay young traveling, keeping physically active, and being social. You must have a good attitude. Age is just a number. They do not let that define them physically, meaning they will not sit in a rocking chair and limit themselves to inactivity just because they are a certain age. They don't feel old and will not act it. Their secret to a good marriage is good communication, respect, and to trust each other. They have had their moments, but they get through it. They laugh and enjoy life together. They are each other's best friend. They don't take each other for granted. They still have a great sex life. Chemistry is important; this can't be overlooked. This is the glue that binds in tough times. A good relationship takes work.

A Morning of Surprises

The next morning, I woke up extra early, eager to take full advantage of my remaining time at the retreat. I fired off a brief email to Thomas then decided to cook everyone breakfast.

It was still dark outside when I ventured into the kitchen, turning on the lights as I went. "What's happening?" said a sleepy Josh, jarred out of dreamland. His golden hair was arranged messily over his face as he hung halfway out of a chair at the table.

"Didn't mean to wake you, hon. Thought I'd come down to cook for all of us today," I whispered.

He scratched his chin lazily. "Oh man, what time is it? Morning already? Alex said there was a girl who arrived last night who was looking for a handsome guy to take her virginity. But I waited up all night and she never came."

I giggled inside myself. "I think someone else might have beaten you to the punch."

"Who?" he said, opening his eyes a little wider.

"Hai, the new guest I met last night. He seemed into her. She seemed...well, you younger bunch have strange ideas about sex." A blanket slid off Josh to reveal chiseled six-pack abs. They were golden brown from days on the beach. I opened the fridge and started cooking. Josh came up behind me and joined in.

"I love a woman who can cook," he said softly in my ear.

"Do you or Alex ever wear shirts?" I joked, cracking some eggs into a big bowl.

"Why, does the gun show bother you? Don't be intimidated by our amazing bodies. We worked hard on them." I couldn't help it; I laughed out loud, mostly from nerves and the fact that Josh's lines were always so cheesy.

"What's funny?" he asked, visibly hurt.

"Nothing, really...sometimes you say the most explicit things," I said, continuing with the slicing of tomatoes.

"They aren't supposed to be funny. They're supposed to be hot," he said, his age showing.

"They are, they are...I mean, for younger women, I'm sure they work very well...."

Josh turned me around by my hips and pulled me against his chest. I found myself wishing that I had worn something more attractive. I was already sporting a stain or two from the cooking. "And what works for you?" he said, gazing into my eyes.

I pushed him away in a friendly manner. "Something far more complicated than abs, I'm afraid," I said.

He leaned behind me and grabbed a slice of toast. "You'll have to teach me about it sometime," he said, his boyish charm leaving with him.

Josh left me alone in the quiet kitchen to finish up my morning cooking fest. I made eggs, bacon, pancakes, and waffles with side salads.

It was a sexually charged morning. Alex came down a while later with Hai, and they shamelessly flirted with me, which put me in a good mood. Gradually, one by one, the others joined us. First Crystal, then Rama and Sita, then Aria and Faith. We all sat at the table eating and drinking, and all was right with the world.

I was in so much pain when I first arrived on Maui. I desperately needed healing, reawakening, and appreciation. I found it all with these people. Each of them was so different yet completely accepting of someone like me. They had made me feel like a part of the family for the short time I had stayed with them.

The seminars and classes that I attended had inspired me. I learned how to meditate and pray like a monk should—I was totally absorbed into their lifestyle and culture. The Maui Magic had seized me, and while there were so many mysteries still to learn, I was slowly coming to terms with the idea that I could learn them all...happy as a single woman.

I lived more in these past few months than I had with Richard in seven years. I did not miss him. I did not miss the constant expectation to be the perfect future wife. And I did not miss the money. Rama stood and glonked a fork down on his plastic cup. Glonk, glonk, glonk... "Oh, anyway, a toast to Katie for this marvelous breakfast," he started.

Surprised, I seized my coffee then realized I was too eager to toast myself. "...and for not taking a card from the bowl this morning. Cheers!"

"Cheers!" came the chorus of familiar voices. Faith added in a whoop or two for good measure. I raised my coffee mug and drank. It was a great feeling to be so appreciated by everyone at the Lotus Retreat.

"Why is it important that I have stopped taking the cards?" I asked Sita a little while after that.

She looked at me like an owl considers its young. "You have stopped putting your faith in the unknown. The cards help you ask the right questions. When you stop needing them, it means you have found some answers."

The Arrival

Just as I was about to explore this nugget of wisdom a bit more, there was a heavy knock on the door. "Got it," shouted Aria, licking her fingers and leaping from the table. I continued chatting to Sita for a few more moments before Aria poked her head back inside the kitchen.

"Aaaah...Katie?"

"Yep?" I asked, wheeling around.

"You have a visitor." Bemused by who it might be, I thought of Jason and the long love texts he had been sending me. I hoped that I could let him down easy this time. I approached the door, attempting to neaten up as I went. Clouds of flour trailed behind me from the pancake mixture, and my white blouse had seen better days. But when I got to the door and it swung open, it was not Jason who stared back at me.

It was Thomas. Airport Thomas. Thomas, the man I had been emailing now for more than two months. The Thomas I had fallen for. Thomas, in person, standing in front of me. "Hello, you," he said, smiling at me. He wore a Hawaiian shirt with blue flowers and a pair of white shorts with white loafers, a classic look that he had executed to perfection.

"Shit!" I said, startled.

"Not quite the reaction I was hoping for, but I'll take it. I hope you don't mind...I wanted it to be a surprise." He reached out and handed me a single red carnation, which I took. Still stunned, I was enveloped in his presence. Six foot tall and as dashing as ever, with his strong jaw and thick, dark hair flecked with gray, he looked like something out of *GQ*.

I was instantly aware that I looked like a kitchen maid. "No, wow, I'm glad to see you," I stammered, loathing my own nerves and wishing that my heart would stop trying to leap from my chest. I leaned forward and hugged him, and he returned it warmly. He still smelled like herbal soap and wood polish. It made my knees quiver.

Imagine feeling two months' of pent up sexual energy converge on you all at once in one of the world's most sexually charged energy spots. "I...I have just been cooking. Please come in. I hope you don't mind if I go upstairs and freshen up?" His eyes were hazel, like two translucent green pools. If lust at first sight exists, this was it.

"Sure, I'll wait," he said, striding inside confidently. Everything about him was delicious. I shot upstairs, passing Faith, who gave me a knowing look, and cleaned myself up. I chose to look sexy casual in shorts and a silk lace-designed tank top. I did not want to look like I was trying too hard, although I did check out my evening gowns several times in the mirror then thought better of it.

I was infatuated, like a teenage girl whose pop idol was downstairs waiting to sweep her off her feet. "Don't be nervous," I kept telling myself, although it was hopeless. A cage of butterflies had been released into my stomach, and they were going crazy. I brushed my hair and applied a bit more makeup then hurried to the stairs and slowed down in the descent.

"This is your chance, Katie. Don't mess it up," my mom's voice said in my mind. All of the emails, the flirting, and the anticipation...I put my shoulders back and arrived on the lower landing like a queen floating into her palace. Thomas stood and brushed himself off as I approached. I liked that I could see some nerves on him as well.

"My lady. Can I offer you lunch somewhere...er...less crowded?" Every eye in the room was on him. I had been talking about Thomas for months. Oh god, I hope no one had said anything.

"Sure, I'd love to," I said.

"We just ate though, so don't be surprised if she's a cheap date," called Faith as we exited the Bamboo Malu House. I could have kicked her.

A Date With Thomas

"It's beautiful here," Thomas said as he opened the car door for me. "You described it well in your emails. Mr. Yamahito gave me some time off for closing the deal. I finally managed to convince some very stubborn designers to sign with us."

I congratulated him, and we drove to Paia for lunch at Milagros on the corner of Baldwin and Hana Highway. We spoke easily, like old kindred spirits picking up where we had left off from our email correspondence. We talked about the progress of my book, and he joked, "Great, your writing pep is starting to pick up steam. Will I be a character in your book? 'I pray he leaves early this weekend' chapter!" We laughed. Lunch eventually turned into dinner, and we chose another spot near the beach, where we could continue talking.

Was I in love with this man? It felt like it. The chemistry was palpable. All I wanted to do was be with him and satisfy my need for intimate love. At what cost though? Throughout the evening, I found out that Thomas was a serious, conservative, intelligent, ambitious man—everything I had ever wanted.

I took him to Secret Beach, a secluded spot in a small cove with the perfect conditions for a midnight swim. After a dip in the ocean, Thomas's shorts clung to him considerably, and we settled on the sand. Then it happened. A long, lingering kiss that blew my heart wide open. His lips were a magnet, and I was powerless against them.

It was a warm Maui night, the moon was out, and the stars reflected in the ocean ahead of us. Rolling tides slid onto the shore then retreated, a hypnotic chorus of love that resonated through both of us. He entwined his fingers in mine as we kissed, sheltering me from the slight wind that was coming in off the ocean.

I was ready. Ready to be taken by this incredible man. I wanted it. I needed it. All thoughts of my vows melted away. How could I ever have been so stupid? I was lost in his embrace. Then, suddenly, he stopped. Clearing his throat, he spoke. "We should be getting back. I don't trust myself with you, Katie. There's something about you...."

I pulled him into another kiss, but he broke it off. "Exactly. Exactly! It feels right. But it's important we take this slowly. You know I just got out of a bad marriage, and I don't want to be the reason you break those vows to yourself. It's not right." I could not believe what I was hearing.

Somehow, he had said what I needed to hear. "I agree," I lied. "Slow is better. Let's, um...take it slow. Slow and steady."

I drove us back while he spoke. I looked over and turned onto our tiny dirt road. I was mesmerized and admired his handsome face and profile, when clunk! We were jolted, and I heard an awful noise as my car sliced over a rock that I knew was on this road—the rock I had been avoiding—but because I was daydreaming and hopelessly in love, or lust, I did not see it. I saw only Thomas, the sexy god, sitting next to me.

I jokingly said, "My god...look what you made me do." We pulled over and discovered the lower part of the car had been ripped and was hanging open. My poor car. Back at the Bamboo Malu House, he joined me in my bedroom. Apparently, sex was off the table, but sleeping together was not. I admit I barely slept that night or the four nights after that.

Thomas's presence at the retreat was incredible, and I devoted all of my time to him. I showed him the temples and the beaches, took him on a jungle walk, and hiked to the bottom of our private 300-foot Hanehoi waterfall that sat near the property. We enjoyed the kissing and hugging that we shared. Rama even did a heart reading for him on his fourth day, although it was strangely strained. Rama's eyes rolled back, his eyelids fluttered, and his lower jaw hung open. He opened his eyes, and after twenty minutes of staring, his verdict was in.

"It's clear that your one eye is lower than the other...how odd," he told Thomas as we sat in the sunny kitchen one morning. With that, he rose and closed the doors to his music room behind him, shooting a suspicious look at Thomas. "I don't think he likes me much," Thomas said, dragging his hand through his dark hair.

"Oh, that's not true. He probably just thinks you are too good looking to be human or something. There are aliens here, you know," I said, dismissing his comment. But when I looked at him now, I noticed that one of his eyes was in fact lower than the other. The following days were pristine, and I was intoxicated with Thomas's presence.

His last night with me came, but something had changed inside me, like a light had been shone on my heart. Since Thomas had arrived, I had stopped writing. I stopped meditating, taking walks, going to the beach to fill my journal with insight, and stopped taking any classes at the Lotus Retreat. I had stopped.

The uneasy feeling had crept in after that comment Rama had left me with. I think he was trying to tell me that no one is perfect. That even Thomas, in all of his sexy, god-like glory, was flawed. I just did not know him well enough yet. Was I ready to delete the life I had started here and throw away all of the progress I had made?

That night I lay with Thomas in bed, and we fooled around. It would have been easy to break my vow. He tried to unbutton my pants, and I found myself stopping him before my thoughts could catch up with me. The words caught in my throat. How did I explain this to him? I desperately wanted him, but I could not do it.

He pulled me closer and stroked my hair. "I want to, but I can't," I said. "If we do this, there is no chance for us. You know it, and I know it. You might be the love of my life, but I'll never find out with so much pain in my heart from my ex. I'll drag you through the mud, and we will lose any chance we ever would have had."

"Timing," he said, nodding gently, "is everything." Things settled down after that, although I could see he was disappointed. After all, he was still a man, and I had been trying to get into his pants all week. He left a while later and said that he would pop back to say goodbye to me in the morning. "I'll never forget this trip," he said as I closed the front door.

I sat at the kitchen table for some time, torn. Did I just let the man of my dreams escape? Had I just ruined the rest of my life? I had to believe that was not the case. If Maui had taught me one thing, it was that men were plentiful. They would always want sex, whether it made sense or not.

All of the men I had dated here were the same. Most of them were tight or had no money, although they were full of ideas. They only wanted someone to listen, who would then satisfy their sexual urges. This was the free love culture I had landed in three months ago. But free love was never really free. It came at a price. That night, I had chosen not to pay the price.

Before retiring to bed, I saw Josh at the kitchen table. "If Thomas breaks up with you, it will be his loss, and I'll marry you," Josh announced.

That young man knew how to make me smile. "I will give you my old jewelry so you can take it apart and make me a wedding ring," I teased.

"I will make you a ring from a palm leaf, and with all your old jewelry, I will make my fiery goddess a tiara." Josh beamed.

Chapter 9

The
Woofers

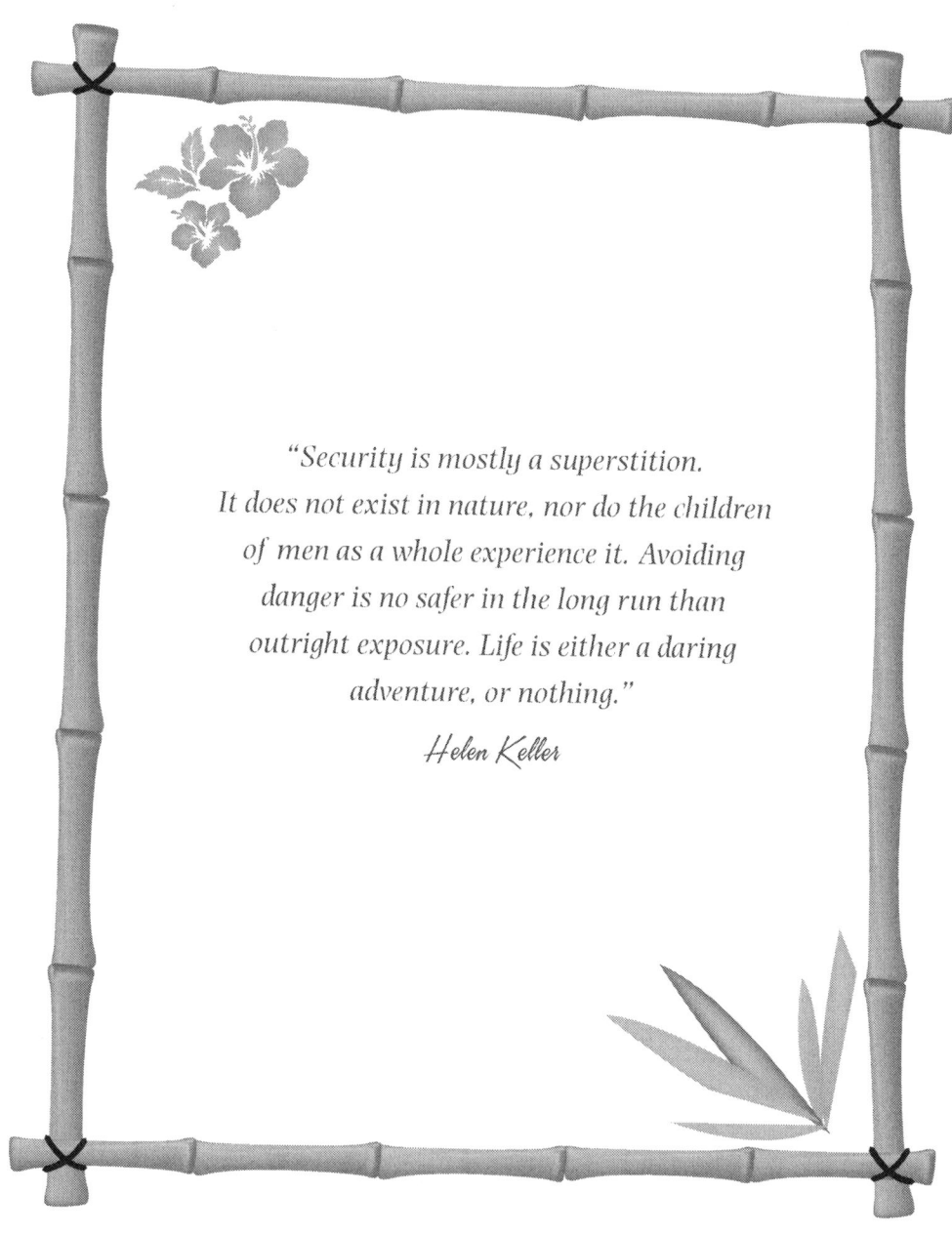

"Security is mostly a superstition.
It does not exist in nature, nor do the children
of men as a whole experience it. Avoiding
danger is no safer in the long run than
outright exposure. Life is either a daring
adventure, or nothing."

Helen Keller

Thomas left the next morning; it was a bittersweet goodbye. I could tell that he was confused about me and not sure why I had refused him the night before. We left on good terms though, and we kissed passionately before he flew back to California. "I'll call you," he said, and he was gone. I wondered if he would.

I remained in my bedroom for the rest of the day, meditating on my decision. The more I thought about it, the more I panicked that I had made the wrong one. It was late afternoon when I finally ventured out to find someone to talk to. Perhaps my friends would be able to shed some light on my situation. Besides, I only had three days left here.

Finding the Right Answers

I descended the stairs and walked into the kitchen in time for a spaghetti dinner. Comfort food, just what I needed. Alex, Josh, Hai, Aria, Crystal, Faith, and the elusive Michael joined us as per Aria's urging. Traveling Shiva Two dropped in for dinner. Everyone contributed to the feast.

"Let's pray and give thanks," Hai announced. We all grabbed hands. He closed his eyes and said, "Bless this food and all of our new friends at this table." Keeping his eyes closed, with a serene smile on his peaceful face, we were all cloaked in silence.

After thirty long, awkward seconds I looked up and caught Aria peeking with one eye. Hai still had his eyes closed and his head bowed. Aria and I made eye contact and smiled at each other. I looked at Hai. Was there more? After twenty more seconds, I decided to break the awkward silence. Hai must be meditating or something. "Okay, everyone, time to eat, amen."

As we finished eating, Sita and Rama joined our table. They would often leave their home and join us at the Bamboo Malu House for meals. Sita spoke. "You are all brave to come to Maui. People talk themselves out of traveling and going after their dreams. They make lots of excuses, but we here know that nothing, not even money, can keep you from a calling." The table dissolved into conversation as Aria and Michael left early to be alone and a few others went out to start a bonfire.

Those of us who remained were in for a treat. "Time for a plate reading," Rama declared. "Do not touch this table; leave everything as it is. Thank you." He started with Alex's plate. "Alex first. You are masculine and feminine and a little empty on top spiritually due to your scientific mind and too much book learning, but you are becoming more spiritually aware here and opening up. Good, good." Then he read my plate. "Katie! You have too much energy. It's all around you in explosions. I have never seen a plate with the knife and fork crossed like a triangle... hmmm." He studied my plate seriously and carefully and picked up again, "Notice how the spaghetti is outside of the triangle. The knife represents male energy and the fork female; the spaghetti is square...." He leaned the plate over to show Sita.

She leaned in to take a closer look at it, "This is good, you have a triangle already. You need to go inside the triangle into your essence. So do not do so much marketing and business outside for a while." She added.

Rama scooped my spaghetti into the triangle and added, "Once you bring the masculine energy inside to be stronger with your feminine energy, then you will be open to receive love and care from others. You, Katie, are an old soul—with many past lives in Egypt."

Next, he picked up Faith's plate. "Many past traumas, fears, and loss...very difficult loss. You are here to receive spiritual healing. You will meet a new man and have another child soon."

Sita and Rama, retreated to their private home on the other side of the property, and Faith retired to her room alone. The remaining dinner party spilled outdoors under the blanketed starry skies. A bonfire was glowing.

"Katie! You have decided to grace us with your presence?" said Hai. I could see he was stoned already.

"You bummed that your dreamboat is gone?" asked Alex in his insightful manner. He was shirtless again, but I was not complaining.

Alex was burning what appeared to be pictures and leaves. "I'm okay that he's gone. What are you guys doing out here?" I asked, noticing that Josh held a batch of pictures of his own.

"We're burning bad memories from the past for spiritual healing," declared Alex, "and enjoying the bonfire of course."

"Want some pot or wine?" offered Crystal, holding out her hand. In it was a small, clear bag with some plant matter inside it. "You smoke it. It is spirit sauce."

"Wine is great, thanks," I said, eyeing the pot suspiciously.

"I'm a space alien!" said Hai, laughing, and for the first time, I noticed how wide his eyes were. His hair was wavier today, but he still looked good.

"I'm sure," I said to him, realizing that Shiva Two, Alex, and I were the only sober people there.

"Spotted any around lately?" I asked, looking from face to face. Crystal nodded vigorously and started scanning the skies above us.

It was strange being around stoned people, but I had no intention of joining them. I was glad for the company. In any event, they stopped asking questions about Thomas, which suited me fine. I was a pincushion of doubts over the last week.

I asked Shiva Two his opinion on love and relationships and Thomas, and he considered me before answering. "Do you want the long answer or the very short one?"

"Either of them is fine, thank you," I told him, eager for his wisdom.

"People often pass on juicy learning opportunities, and they miss everyday miracles even though they are all around us. Recognizing them and being spontaneous is what life is about. My advice is to stop thinking about Thomas. He is not on Maui. I am here with you at a wonderful picture burning ceremony. Enjoy our moments together. Live in this juicy moment."

Hai, Josh, and Shiva Two got along extremely well. For most of the next hour, I listened to them talk about conspiracy theories. "We all walk on the same ground; we are all flesh and blood. We should not worship gurus. No one person is better than another. We should worship only God and no one else," responded Hai insightfully. "Maybe we will even see aliens tonight," he added with a sparkle in his eye.

At the rate they were going, I was surprised that they were not seeing them already. Crystal passed around a bong with pot in it, and again I refused. It was interesting watching them, but some things did not make any sense. At one point Alex insisted that angels were aliens, and a debate broke out.

Hai was a peaceful guy. I noticed that he spoke in code and had a habit of leaving his comments open ended, expecting me and others to understand what he was thinking. I found it irritating. "Those chemtrails are poisoning everyone," he said, arranging himself on a rock in a meditative position to gather supernatural energy, palms up, at the ready. He was crazy about organic farming, a very passionate man. I have always admired men with the vision to create products and companies. Many of us here on the island believe, we need to be more self-sufficient and grow our own organic fruit and vegetables instead of imported food, and to avoid GMOs and pesticides.

We spoke about power spots on the earth and other fascinating mystical beliefs. "I believe that Maui and Huelo Lookout is an energy spot; that is why I booked a room here," Hai told us. I would later come to find that many people believe that Lemuria existed and that it had been somewhere among the islands.

"Lemuria was a huge continent though," Hai continued. "It covered most of the South Pacific and the ring of fire islands. These are the mountaintops of this lost continent." The evening wore on, and we spoke about God and religion in detail. "Do not worship these gurus or leaders. We all walk on the same ground. We are flesh and blood."

"Didn't you say that already?" I started to say before Josh chimed in, "And I definitely believe in aliens—and I'm not talking about the illegal kind," he added.

"Aliens? I don't know about that," I commented, not for the first time.

"No really, we are a three dimensional world, but the planet is going through a lot of changes, and as it does this, we are going to enter into another dimension completely," Josh said. Hai agreed with him. I wondered if I had aliens in the form of Josh and Hai sleeping down the hall from me.

"And we are all turning crystalline," Josh threw in as if that closed the matter.

"These are pretty out-there opinions," I said carefully, thinking.

"Yeah, but you gotta believe in something. Lemuria and Atlantis, these are cool things to believe in," Josh said, sipping on his drink. "I also believe that angels are weighed down on Earth and walk among us—that we are all connected," he said.

Hai agreed. They were a pair of very interesting guys. "I believe if you open up spiritually, you will see them too." Feeling uncomfortable about the direction of the conversation, I steered it in a new direction by asking Hai some personal questions.

"This is my girlfriend, yeah—she lives in New York. She is my twin flame. We have known each other for about a year and met through an organization online that believes in Lemuria and Atlantis. We met for the first time in person here on Maui. I can't wait to see her again in New York," Hai finished.

Eventually, the others retired to bed, and it was only Josh, Hai, and I left. They were both very interested in what I was saying. I could feel the sexual energy mounting.

"I had better get to bed, guys. It's been a long day," I announced as Hai moved closer to me still. I said goodnight and wandered off back to my room. I stripped and pulled on my t-shirt and sweatpants and put in my mouth guard, preparing to climb into bed. There were no emails from Thomas, but why should there be? He was probably still jetlagged from the plane trip.

I snuggled into bed, put on a movie, and watched it on my laptop. About an hour later, a gentle rap on my door woke me from an uneasy slumber. "Katie? Hey, Katie? It's me, Hai."

I slid off my bed and pressed my ear up against the door. "Hai? What's up?" I whispered back to him. The night was pressing into my bedroom, and all noise had died out outside. It must have been one in the morning.

"Can I come in and cuddle with you?" he asked.

The nerve! It is strange to feel flattered and insulted at the same time, but that is how I felt. I opened the door a crack and could not speak clearly with my plastic mouthpiece. "No, that's not a good idea," I said, feeling tempted. It would have been only too easy to open the door. What was I thinking? "No," I repeated firmly.

"Don't get the wrong idea. I don't want sex, just some cuddling. I could feel you needed it earlier. I am here for you," he said. Smooth.

"Thanks, but I'm fine. I don't want it to lead to anything," I whispered to him. My bulky mouth guard and baggy sleepwear did not seem to deter him.

"I just want to watch the sun rise with you. I don't mind that you are older. You are gorgeous."

"Hai, I appreciate the flattery, but no thanks. I'm going back to bed now. Didn't you say you had a girlfriend?"

"Yes, I do, but we have an open relationship."

"Hai, you should be faithful to her. I will see you in the morning." I locked my door, went back to bed, and that was that.

The old me would have found him very appealing, but I no longer needed a man's attention to feel good about myself. I was far better off keeping things simple and enjoying my final days at the retreat.

The next morning, I skipped breakfast. Josh was there with Alex and Hai, and I felt awkward about the night before. I could see he was a little embarrassed by it. I grabbed some almond butter, a banana, and coconut juice freshly chopped from the tree and headed straight to the temple. Time to continue with my writing. I made the journey to the smaller temple and settled down to some meditation.

I wrote:

I learned a new term yesterday. FOB means 'Fresh Off the Boat'; not sure, but I think this phrase has many meanings, like fresh catch of the day, wet behind the ears, or doesn't have her Maui legs yet. The men are particularly attracted to women who are FOB I notice. An FOB person is new to the island. The official Hawaiian word, malihini, also means newcomer to Hawaii.

Alex shared his belief with me that physical symptoms of an illness appear "after" we experience trauma or when a negative emotional trigger is activated in our lives. It is an emotional release or "cause and effect." After living a life of stress for so long, it can alter your cells, your chemistry. He said it is actually a good sign when the physical symptoms come to surface so you can recognize something is wrong. Then the real healing can begin when brought to the light. You need to face the emotional cause or root that caused the illness. The more obvious symptoms happen during repair, like lethargy and pain. These are beneficial in that they clearly identify what part/organ of the body has been affected, and from that, we can work with the specific, correlated stress to ensure that it is resolved. Recurrent symptoms, or chronic problems, are the result of encountering an emotional trigger that causes us to revisit the old situation that caused us the initial stress.

I put down my journal and tried to meditate; it was useless. Once again those intrusive thoughts invaded my mind. Did I do the right thing with Thomas? Was I blowing off important experiences with other men because of him? I opened my eyes and relaxed back on the temple wall. Surrounded by nature, I felt completely isolated. Then I saw it—a note from Sita perched on the goddess statue.

Lessons in Love

I opened it carefully and read,

Dearest Katie, Your time with us is almost over. Take some time to think about your experiences here and what they have taught you. I hope you have enjoyed it here; you will always have a place with us. I'm glad you kept the promise you made to yourself. Aloha.

P.S.: I took the liberty of drawing your final card for you.

How did she know? I wondered, but then, it was Sita. Mysterious wisdom was her thing. I checked the envelope again, and there was my final card. Taking a deep breath, I drew it out.

"Home," it said.

My eyes welled up with tears as I stood there holding my life in my hands. No other card could have spoken to me like this one did. It was everything to me. After all I had been through, my struggle for a new independent life, this had been my only desire since I had left the islands as a small child.

It was true. I had rediscovered my home here. If I had been with Thomas, who knows where I may have ended up? It would have turned my happiness here inside out. Since I had arrived, I had moved from man to man, searching for something I could not understand.

Now I knew that thing I had longed for was home. I felt at peace here at the Lotus Retreat because everyone had made me feel welcome. They had shown me once again what a home could be, what it really felt like to live among friends and equals.

It was time that I embraced this place and everything in it to live the life I deserved. I was not planning on going to the bonfire that night, but the decision was easy now. Why should I not go? Because Hai was going? Because Josh would be there? Because I might see Jason and a few of the other men I had dated since arriving?

What nonsense. Why deprive myself of the very thing that makes me happy for the sake of potential approval from a man? I hurried back to the Bamboo Malu House to mix up some mean cosmopolitan cocktails for the beach bonfire. Everyone had to bring something, and I was always rather excellent at a cocktail mix.

Bonfires and Beyond

The Bamboo Malu House was alive with activity. Everyone was excited to attend the bonfire that night. It was held at the remote beach down the cliff, and anyone could attend. It was a warm, muggy evening when we all arrived in unison for the festivities. The sun was descending over the jade colored mountains tinting the passing clouds orange and magenta, and once the boys had stacked the wood and lit the fire, the air smelled like coals and love.

Faith had brought Pollyanna the parrot, Sita's pet, whom she had grown close to over the last week of my absence. She had taught it to say the most incredible things. Whenever I approached, it would launch into a fit of "Love is all you need, squawk, love is all you need."

My cocktails were a hit as expected, Alex proclaiming me the best Cosmo mixologist he had ever known. With the last of the light, I decided to go for a quick beach run. My newfound freedom demanded it, and I would deny myself no longer. I took off barefoot at a steady pace, streaking down the wet, sandy beach.

My heart thudding in my chest, I stopped to watch the last inklings of light fleck the sky before they faded away. Once again, I was here—in the place that made me happiest—the wet sand squelching between my toes. Everything was right in the world. Well, almost everything.

I looked back down the beach at my friends and island family. They had taught me the meaning of the Aloha spirit. Each one of them had a smile on their faces. Sure, they had flaws. They were fighting the battle of life as hard as anyone. But they had found something more here—a community, a spirit of oneness that made fallibility a precious thing.

Inspired by the dancing flames, I pulled out my phone in the darkness and was pleased to find that there was reception here. I immediately dialed Thomas. It rang five times before he answered, breathless. "Hi, Thomas, just wanted to thank you for coming to visit me again," I said, a slight wind ruffling my hair.

"Hey, Katie! I had a good time with you, sure. How's the island?"

he said in a strained voice.

"Incredible," I said, honestly embracing the fundamental truth of that statement. "It was the best decision I ever made coming back here."

"That's great...listen, can I call you back sometime? I'm a little...uh...preoccupied at the moment."

I heard the sound of a woman's voice in the room with him. Surprisingly, I felt no hostility, only love. "Sure...and Thomas?"

"Yeah?" he said.

"Have fun." I hung up the phone and was delighted to find that I meant it. We were not dating. Why shouldn't he be with someone else? I had been dating other men. At least he was happy.

How profound that moment felt. In the past, hearing another woman's voice would have crippled me. I would have blamed myself, told myself that if I had only been with him, he never would have had to look for someone else.

In my heart, I knew I had done the right thing. Thomas was a friend. Maybe one day, when we are both ready, it could develop into something else. But the timing was all wrong. I had a lot of life left to live, and Maui was the place to live it.

I owed it to myself and to any man I would spend my life with to be my own person when he met me—to know who I was and what I wanted. Love should never feel like a chore. I had to tend to my own garden before tending to someone else's—otherwise, they would both die.

Maui had shown me that self-sacrifice neither encouraged love nor caused it to endure. I walked back to the bonfire and grabbed a fresh Cosmo with my friends and island family (ohana). The boys were all painting their faces blue.

"What does the blue face mean?" I asked Sita. Tribal music was drifting through the bonfire, and everyone was swaying in motion to its intensity.

"It's Rama's way of reconnecting with the whale—they are in season," she said. "It's the closest he has ever felt with nature. It helps him relax and explore his spiritual connection with the world."

"Wonderful," I said sitting serenely by the fire.

"You look happy, Katie. Things have worked out for you here," Sita commented. Not a question but a statement.

"They definitely have. Thank you for the note in the temple this morning. I appreciate all that you have done to teach me and guide me to this healing place."

Faith blundered onto our log and squeezed a chair between us. "Where's Pollyanna?" asked Sita.

"She's off...um, reconnecting with her spiritual side," she said, looking nervous.

Sita hurried off in the direction Faith had pointed out. "You let her fly away, didn't you?" I giggled.

"She's a bird; birds fly. She'll be back. How are you holding up? Was that Thomas on the line? Saw you chatting over there in no man's land."

"It was, it was," I confessed. "We're staying friends. Neither of us is ready for anything serious."

Faith looked impressed. "Wow, look at you. I was half preparing myself for an early December wedding. Good for you, Katie."

"Oh shit, here comes Aria. Quick, look busy," Faith declared pretending to play an imaginary guitar and she started humming a song she composed.

Aria was holding out a plate of fresh fruit and vegetables from our garden and smiled at me as I took one. "That's awesome... after that, it's time to dance," she said.

"Nooo," Faith complained, helping herself to more natural sweetness.

"Yes, it will be as good as you pretending to play your imaginary guitar" said Aria as she spun around, balancing the plate on a nearby rock, and started dancing with the boys.

The music was melodic and inviting, and I longed to join in. "You should dance," I said to Faith while finishing my papaya.

"What's the point? You're just leaving soon, aren't you? Then I'll be stuck in this paradise with no one to complain to."

"I'm moving to the other side of the island, Faith," I declared, "not back to California."

"What? Yea! So we can still go out together?" she asked, beaming.

"As long as I can drive," I joked.

Faith pulled me into a hug, heart to heart, and stood. "Okay then. Let's do it."

The moon was high, and the stars were bright. In the middle of the beach, a bonfire raged. Around it were some people embracing the freedom of island life. The trees rustled as we danced in the darkness, a plume of light and connected hearts.

The music thrummed rhythmically, a drumbeat that echoed through the world. My eyes were closed, but my heart was open. I danced alone but surrounded by friends. I tasted the salt of the ocean in my mouth, and the joy of independence in my body.

I danced for myself. It did not matter that my future was uncertain or that I did not have answers for the coming days. All that mattered was this moment. I fell into the beat, flickering with the flames. Rama grabbed Sita, and they swayed gloriously as he curled his arms around his beloved.

Crystal and Faith dashed around the fire, showing off for the boys. Aria and Michael slow danced, lost in each other's eyes. I was at peace, happy for the first time since I had left Richard. The pain in my heart was gone, replaced with a newfound love and appreciation for myself.

For now, I was with myself and happy to be here. The thought enveloped me like the warmth from the flames. Our circle grew wider as more people joined from outside the farm. It didn't matter. We were all after the same thing: freedom and joy.

I had learned a lot from that mystical place in the jungle; it had been the best Maui magical, mystical tour. Sometimes the most alien thing in your life can be your own thoughts. Strange things happen that you would never want to explain. Everyone deserves love and consideration.

I was a new woman, with the world unfurling like a flower ahead of me. I could do anything. It turns out that sometimes the hardest battle to win is the one raging in your own heart. When that happens, you can either take the journey seriously, or succumb to the obstacles in your path that keep you stagnant and wanting. Change starts inside.

I found what I was looking for on Maui—the perfect place for me to pray, play, and love. I found what I needed—family, attention, creativity—and I discovered that sometimes Faith, although it can drive you crazy, can also be your best friend.

References

Acknowledgements

Photo credit: authors image back cover and About the Author by Alek Mikolajczyk, www.vipalekmiko.com

Chapter 1

Hawaii in the Words of Mark Twain, http://www.hawaiishrine.com/mtwain.htm

Chapter 2

Emma Lazarus Poem, "The New Colossus," https://news.google.com/newspapers?nid=1144&dat=19810124&id=LN4cAAAAIBAJ&sjid=GWMFAAAAIBAJ&pg=4590,3155899&hl=en

Chapter 3

Paul Gauguin Quote, BrainyQuote, http://www.brainyquote.com/quotes/quotes/j/joelosteen579070.html

Chapter 4

Lindbergh, Anne Morrow, Gift From the Sea, Page 79.

Chapter 5

Gauguin, Paul, Noa Noa: The Tahitian Journal, Page 12.

Chapter 6

Helen Keller Quotes, BrainyQuote, http://www.brainyquote.com/quotes/quotes/h/helenkelle101301.html

Chapter 7

Anonymous Quote, BrainyQuote, http://www.brainyquote.com/quotes/quotes/m/marktwain120156.html

Chapter 8

Walt Disney Quotes, BrainyQuote, http://www.brainyquote.com/quotes/quotes/w/waltdisney132637.html

Chapter 9

Helen Keller Quotes, BrainyQuote, http://www.brainyquote.com/quotes/quotes/h/helenkelle121787.html

Artwork Details

Front cover
**Don't Mess With My World,
It Is All I Got**
Oil on canvas, 30" x 40"

Introduction
Kauai Magic
*30"X30" - on metal mixed
medium. Acrylic paint, oil paint,
and clear coat*

Chapter 1
Childhood Expressions
*Sparkling Spreckelsville Shores
16"×20" on metal mixed
medium. Acrylic paint, oil paint,
and clear coat*

Chapter 2
Spiritual Calling
*Seven Sacred Falls, Hana Maui
24"×36" on metal mixed
medium. Acrylic paint, oil paint,
and clear coat.*

Chapter 3
The Lotus Retreat
*French Polynesia Paradise
Dwelling
Oil on canvas, 18" x 24"*

Chapter 4
A Forest of Tantra
Maui Vision
Oil on canvas, 12" x 24"

Chapter 5
Finding a New Home
Dream on...Until Your Dream Comes True
24"×31,75" on metal mixed medium. Acrylic paint, oil paint, and clear coat

Chapter 6
Mother Maui
Whale Lullaby, Makena Beach, Maui
24"×24" on metal mixed medium. Acrylic paint, oil paint, and clear coat.

Chapter 7
Dancing With Yourself
Reflection
Oil on canvas, 18" x 24"

Chapter 8
Dinner With Faith
Secret Beach Make a Wish
18"×24" on metal mixed
medium. Acrylic paint, oil paint,
and clear coat.

Chapter 9
The Woofers
New Life - Rebirth
24"×32" on metal mixed
medium. Acrylic paint, oil paint,
and clear coat.

About the Author

Kathy McCartney is the owner of Maui Vision Rentals. Maui Vision became a reality and a business starting with Ms. McCartney's condo, C618. The idea to start her own business came about while working for her friends Sharene and Harrison Klein of Hawaii-Holiday. The Klein's have been a guiding force in helping Kathy get started with her own vacation rental business.

When she was a young girl, Kathy lived on the island of Oahu with her U.S. Naval family. Her family later moved to Southern California. She knew one day she would return to Hawaii, the place she fell in love with long ago. Kathy has over 25 years of business administration and customer service experience working for large corporations and high-tech start-ups. Taking a leap of faith, she purchased her Maui condo in June of 2002. This was the beginning of fulfilling her prophecy to once again return to Hawaii.

Kathy is a tropical artist residing on Maui. She is inspired by the beauty and romance of the islands. Kathy's fine art paintings are executed on canvas and most recently on etched metal. Photographs of her art can only capture a portion of the must-see pieces, which appear 3D, vibrating and dancing with the surrounding light.

To find where her art is on display and for sale, visit:
www.McCartneyFineArt.com

Looking for clean, comfortable and beautiful accommodations on Maui, visit:
www.MauiVision.com

Linked In:
https://www.linkedin.com/in/kathy-mccartney-204454

Visit the links below for McCartney paintings, photos, fun facts, articles, and news about Maui and the Hawaiian Islands:

Blog:
http://mccartneytropicalexpressions.blogspot.ca/

Facebook:
https://www.facebook.com/MauiVisionRentals/
https://www.facebook.com/McCartneyFineArts/?fref=ts

Instagram:
https://www.instagram.com/mauivisionrent/

Pinterest:
https://www.pinterest.com/kathym1658/

Twitter:
https://twitter.com/MauiVisionRent

YouTube Channel – Kathy McCartney:
https://www.youtube.com/user/TheHawaiikat

Made in the USA
San Bernardino, CA
22 March 2018